Africa
A Land of Hope

By Donna Ward

DONNA WARD
NORTHWOODS PRESS

This book is dedicated to Murray and Beverly Taylor and their three outstanding children,
Zachary, Victoria, and Nicholas, with whom we had such great fun
on our African adventure. May their love for God impact many
and impart hope for generations to come.

I wish to thank the people who contributed to this project including: Rod Forrest, Aaron Gonyou, Wilma Morrison, Compassion Canada staff, Compassion Kenya staff, and project directors. Particular gratitude is extended to the Taylor family. Appreciated editors are: David and Irene Herbert, Tony and Mary Kamau (Kenyan), Francis and Bernadette Kabango (Rwandan), and Dorothy Apedo-Clarke (Ugandan). Thanks to Robert Vaughan and Ashley Morrison. Extra appreciation is extended to my home team: my parents, Marjorie and Elmer Cassidy, for repeated readings; my husband, Douglas, for constant support; Jeremy, Stephanie, and Darcy who put up with my Africa obsession for the last few years and Natalie and Stefan for passionately supporting nine sponsored children and motivating us to sponsor more. Most importantly, recognition is offered to the struggling children of Africa whose tenacity, courage, and hope during hardship inspires us to action and humbles our hearts.

Photo Credits:

Care has been taken to trace ownership of copyright materials contained in this book. Information enabling the publisher to rectify and reference or credit in future editions will be welcome.

pages 7 (lion), 9 (lion), 37, 40, 42, 43, 44 Donna Ward
pages 7 (children), 8, 9 (gorilla) courtesy of Robert Dell
pages 11, 12, 19 (crocodile), 31 (gorilla) courtesy of Robert Dell
page 10 cc by sa, Harald Süpfle
page 13 GFDL, Jaakko Sakari Reinikainen
pages 15 (desert), 17 (tuareg) cc by sa, Florence Devouard
pages 5, 15 (map), 23, 31 NASA
page 16 courtesy of Linus Ågren
page 17 (Oasis) GFDL, Volker Scherl
page 18 (canal), 49 (Mandela), USFG
page 18 (Sphinx) cc by sa, Ian Sewell
page 19 (Camel) courtesy of Nick Fraser
page 20 Stefan Goertz
page 21 courtesy of Erik Kristensen
page 24 cc by sa, Wendy Cain, (sign) cc by sa, Andy Wright
page 25 (Etching) PD
page 25 (Johnson-Sirleaf) Government of Liberia

page 26 cc by sa, Zubro
page 29 GFDL, Brian Smithson
page 32 Tornasole
page 33 PD
page 34 GFDL, Michael Rosenberg
page 35 ILO
page 36 courtesy of AdBusters
page 39 (elephants) cc by sa, M. Disdero, (Great Rift) Douglas Ward
page 44 Compassion International
page 45 cc by sa, Tjeerd Wiersma
page 47 courtesy of Brian McMorrow
page 48 fair use, Robert Hoffman
page 49 (Soweto Township) cc by 2.0 Matt-80
page 50 GFDL, Mario Sarto
page 51 Jeremy Ward
page 52 Victoria Taylor

Cover designed by Adam Duguay, Images
Printed and bound in Canada

Published by Donna Ward/Northwoods Press
www.donnaward.net   info@donnaward.net

Library and Archives Canada Cataloguing in Publication

Ward, Donna, 1958-
        Africa, a land of hope / by Donna Ward.

Includes bibliographical references.
ISBN-13: 978-0-9686788-4-8
ISBN-10: 0-9686788-4-X

        1. Africa—Textbooks.   I. Title.

DT3.W37 2007   960   C2006-906640-X

Table of Contents

Introduction

I have traveled all over the world—in my mind. In Africa, most school children work with very limited supplies—few books and definitely no internet access. With all our resources, we have the world at our fingertips. Pull up a comfy chair. I want to take you to exotic places, clamoring markets, jungle swamps, and crowded slums. Is there an African who does not have rhythm? Soak up the music! Immerse yourself in films, photos, and stories. For those of you who do someday visit Africa, you will go to a place you know.

The ministry of Compassion has helped my family gain some understanding of the life of a child in need. We realize how blessed we are, but also the great responsibility of helping the needy. The integrity of Compassion has been apparent in its administration and on the field. We have personally seen the great love, commitment, and skill of social workers and church leaders at the projects. This help has extended beyond hope for the children to hope for families. We have seen whole families find freedom in Jesus because one child became involved with the local church through sponsorship. We have witnessed Compassion sponsored children who have broken out of poverty and are now sponsors themselves! Through this study we believe that your children will not only learn about Africa, but their values will be challenged. We trust that they will break away from consumerism to become life-long contributors to God's work around the world.

Using This Study Guide

Symbols:

 Read a selection of a printed or web-based resource.

Specified notebook work (either paper or electronic).

 Corresponding Episode on the *Africa, A Land of Hope* DVD

Websites have been carefully selected to bring your children the highest quality of information. Link easily through donnaward.net. Every effort will be made to keep the links active and updated.

Resources:
- Internet: Search using the words in bold to find the site, or go to donnaward.net for easy links.
- Additional resources are vital to making this a "living" study.
- Look along library shelves for titles not otherwise listed.
- The adult section will contain oversized photographic publications.
- Nature films/books are in the 570s.
- African geography is found in 916.
- Resources listed in the first chapter are suitable for the entire study.
- Contact Donna with your feedback, favorite titles, and internet sites for future inclusions.

Notebooks:
- Can become valuable keepsakes.
- Reinforce learning.
- Show a record of study.
- See reproducible maps and notebook pages in Chapter VII.
- Keep a list of favorite books, films, and websites; students will want to come back to them another time.

Hint for notebooks: Copyright permission is not needed to put pictures from websites, such as country flags or wildlife, in unpublished student projects or for personal study use. Right click on picture, choose *Save As,* and save in an electronic folder for insertion on a notebook page. See Easylinks at **donnaward.net** for detailed instructions.

Africa, A Land of Hope - DVD:
Episode 1–Welcome to Africa
Episode 2–The Need for Water
Episode 3–SODIS
Episode 4–Jackie
Episode 5–Legacy of Dreams Fulfilled
Episode 6–Rwandan Diary
Episode 7–A Visit to Kenya
Episode 8–Hunger in the Slums
Episode 9–A New Generation of Leaders
Episode 10–A Picture of Care
Supplementary Segments

The Continent

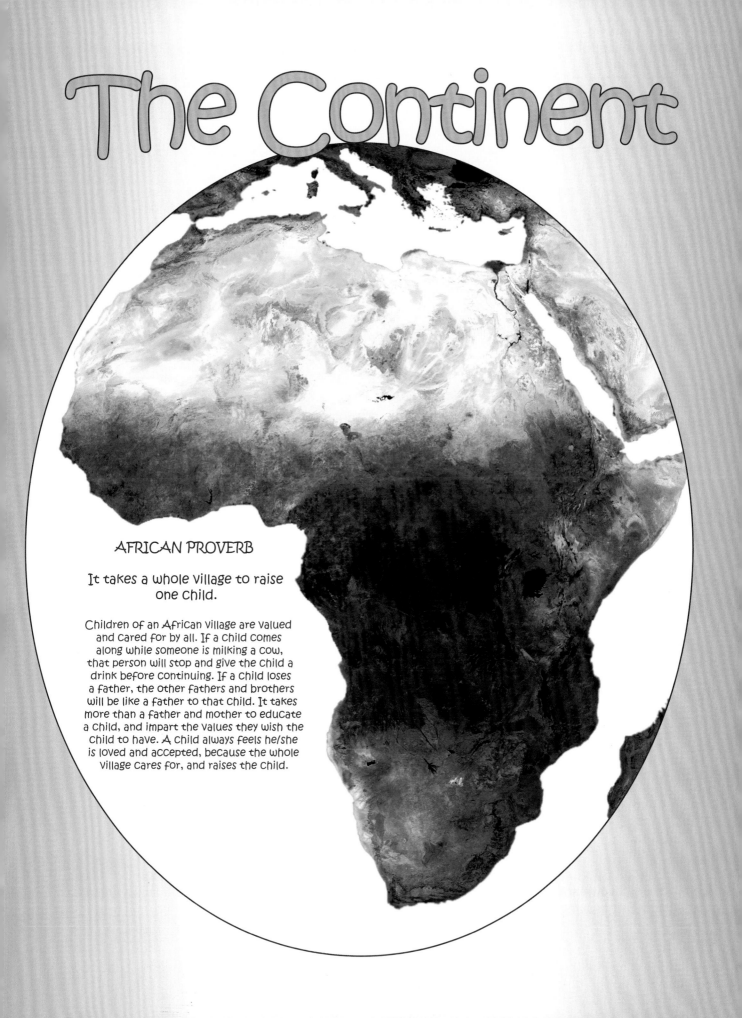

AFRICAN PROVERB

It takes a whole village to raise
one child.

Children of an African village are valued
and cared for by all. If a child comes
along while someone is milking a cow,
that person will stop and give the child a
drink before continuing. If a child loses
a father, the other fathers and brothers
will be like a father to that child. It takes
more than a father and mother to educate
a child, and impart the values they wish the
child to have. A child always feels he/she
is loved and accepted, because the whole
village cares for, and raises the child.

Resources

Internet:
Easylinks and updates for the following websites at donnaward.net

Internet Maps Sites:
Sheppard Software. My favorite site. Free map games with high-speed or dial-up versions.
Mapmaker, Mapmaker, Make Me a Map. Excellent!
World Atlas. All kinds of maps, flags of the world etc.
How Far is It? by Indo. Choose two locations and calculate the distance.
Feeding Minds. Follow link to World Hunger Map.

Internet Geography Sites:
Mr. Dowling's Electronic Passport. Follow links to Africa.
Times Around the World, Clarinet. What time is it in Africa? Search for local times around the world.
Geographia. Good for beginning explorations.
Students Around the World. Information about countries; some with photo tabs.
The Africa Guide, Map of Africa.
About Geography.
Odyssey World Trek. A great site of a group who treks all over Africa. Check out music clips and extra pages.
National Geographic. Lots of resources to look through.
The Story of Africa, BBC World Service. British Broadcasting site with great information.

Internet News Sites:
All Africa. Excellent for current events. Search by country or topic for latest reports from African newspapers.
National Public Radio. Listen to Jason Beaubien's excellent 5 part radio series *Africa's Lagging Development*.

Internet Photo Sites:
A Day in the Life of Africa. Select a morning, midday, or evening slide show and look at the photos with a map handy to find the countries pictured (Book by same title available).
Travelers & photographers who post their photos online.

Bernard Cloutier	**Flickr** (Many photographers. Search by subject.)	
Galen R. Frysinger	**Dan Heller**	**Hans Hendriksen**
Brian McMorrow	**On the Matrix**	

Books:
Cohen, David. *A Day in the Life of Africa.* Amazing oversize photos from the same day across the continent.
Croze, Harvey. *Africa for Kids, Exploring a Vibrant Continent.* In depth and informative.
Martell, Hazel Mary. *Exploring Africa.* Colorful. Highly Recommended. Out of Print.
See your library for many more. Look in Adults & Children:Travel - 916.7, History/Geography - 960,
        Wildlife 591.5-599

Films:
National Geographic nature films of African wildlife (various titles, check your library).
National Geographic Africa. Eight episodes in four DVDs. Highly recommended.

Music:
Check your library. Many titles available.
My Favorites:

Ladysmith Black Mambazo introduced the world to the beauty of black South African harmony; the extraordinary style is known generically as mbube. Lead singer Joseph Shabalala and this close-knit family have entertained and praised God for over 25 years. They performed in the Disney movie, "The Lion King II."

Hope, Hugh Maskela. Escaping the oppression of South Africa in 1960, Hugh Maskela brought his African jazz trumpet style to North America and Europe. Maskela plays South African music in its truest contemporary form. He brings music of hope and understanding for those in the townships, barracks and backwoods of South Africa. If you like jazz, you will love this album.

View *Africa, A Land of Hope*: Episode 1 - Welcome to Africa.

What do you know about the continent of Africa? What is the land like? What wildlife live there? Do you know the names of any countries? Africa is a vibrant, exciting continent—full of extremes; full of adventure.

Look at some photographs of Africa and come up with a list of questions you have about the continent and the people who live there. What are the things you wonder about?

Africa is a place of extreme landscapes, from the largest desert in the world to hot, steamy jungles. The grasslands are home to unique, exotic animals. There are over fifty countries, many overlapping cultures, and several thousand ethnic groups. There is a distinction between North African countries which largely associate themselves with Arabic culture and *sub*-Saharan countries, meaning countries *below* the Sahara Desert.

Africa contains well over a thousand languages! Perhaps closer to two thousand! It is common to find individuals in Africa who not only speak several African languages fluently, but also several European ones as well.

The people of Africa have to contend with illnesses not experienced in the developed world, such as malaria and sleeping sickness. Governing the people of Africa is complicated since national borders unequally divide tribal lands. These issues, combined with corrupt governments and problems from colonialism, have caused Africa to be the poorest continent in the world today.

African countries are quite young as countries go; less than fifty years! National unity and success often takes a long time. There is much poverty, war, and disease in Africa, but there is also hope, courage, and love that bursts forth in the midst of all these troubles. Come on a journey to discover the geography and spirit of Africa. May your knowledge be broadened and your heart enlarged.

What is a Developing Country?
Developing countries are low and middle-income countries. Nearly all the people have a lower standard of living and access to fewer goods and services than do most people in high-income countries. The majority of African countries are considered developing countries. The term *Third World* was used several decades ago to describe the lower income countries of Africa, Asia, Latin America and Oceania. This term is considered by some as outdated.

Money matters. It has the potential to be used for greatness, but it can also be used in hurtful ways. Money is powerful. Solomon says in Ecclesiastes, "Wisdom is a shelter as money is a shelter, but the advantage of knowledge is this: that wisdom preserves the life of its possessor." What do you think this means?

You will be making a paper or electronic notebook as you study Africa.

Choose your option. Create a title page which includes title, your name, month, year, and an illustration.
Also create a resources page to record all your favorite books, films, and internet sites. Make columns for the title, date, and author.

Location in the World

📖 Look at a map of Africa in a picture atlas and discuss points of interest.

Absolute Location

The *absolute location* describes where a place is by the exact degrees of longitude and latitude. Use an atlas to read about hemispheres, longitude, and latitude.

Find the following:

*   Is the landmass of Africa mostly in the eastern or western hemisphere?
*   What line of latitude crosses through the centre of Africa?
*   Name other important lines of latitude.

Compassion Canada President, Barry Slauenwhite, poses in fun at the equator marker in Uganda.

Note the letters on the Equator marker showing south and north. Decide if the photographer is facing east or west. In which direction is Mr. Slauenwhite looking? Do you think this picture was taken in the morning or the afternoon? Why?

Relative Location

The *relative location* of a place describes its location with reference to other places.

Look at the atlas and find the country of Namibia. The relative location of Namibia is southwest Africa bordered on the west by the Atlantic Ocean. It is just north of South Africa, south of Angola, and west of Botswana.

Find and name the seven continents on a world map. Describe the relative location of the continent of Africa by identifying the following:

*   Africa is east of which two continents?
*   Africa is south of which continent?
*   Africa is west of which continent?
*   Africa is north of which continent?

What does the term poverty really mean? Poverty has been defined as not having enough money to enjoy a reasonable standard of life. But what is a reasonable standard of life? The definition varies from one country to another. For example, some people think poverty means not owning a car and a T.V. In Africa, these would be signs of wealth.

Perhaps the true definition of poverty is not having sufficient means to provide for basic human needs, such as adequate and nutritious food, clothing, housing, clean water, health services, and education (moderate poverty) or food alone (extreme poverty).

Why are people poor? Poverty in developing nations can be the result of war, poor government, or disease; but mostly it is because a person is born into poverty. Poverty breeds poverty. The cycle is not easily broken. People who grow up in an impoverished culture lack the nutrition, education, and opportunity to change their own circumstances.

Answer: The photographer is facing west. Mr. Slauenwhite is looking east. The picture was taken in the late morning because the sun is in the east shining down on Mr. Slauenwhite's face. It is creating a shadow behind the marker.

 Notebook: Using a ruler and your atlas, draw the following lines of latitude on your Political Map: Equator, Tropic of Capricorn, Tropic of Cancer. Enjoy an online map game to learn the countries of Africa or read a book.

📖 Look at photographs of the landscapes of Africa either in a book or online.

Desert

Three African deserts cover a large portion of the continent. The Sahara Desert, in the north, is the largest desert in the world. The Kalahari Desert, in the south, receives some rainfall which supports grasses, thorny shrubs, and Acacia trees. Vegetation keeps the sand dunes from shifting and thus the Kalahari could actually be called a dry savanna. Along the south-Atlantic coast, the parched Namib Desert has endless orange dunes blown into razor sharp ridges by the wind. The dunes are some of the highest in the world. Each year the Sahara and Kalahari Deserts slowly creep closer together as desert sands blow and cover fertile ground.

Rainforest

The tropical rainforest is a hot, moist region found along the equator. The temperature stays the same year round and averages around 25°C/77°F in the day. Vegetation grows quickly and thickly. The green, leafy canopy spreads like a roof far above the ground, keeping the jungle floor steamy and dim. The rainforest supports an amazing array of wildlife. The transitional zone between the tropical rainforest and the savanna is a tropical forest which has warm, dry periods between rainy seasons.

Gorillas are the largest of the primate family and they live in the tropical rain forest.

Sahel

The area between the Sahara Desert and the fertile grasslands of the south is called the Sahel, an Arabic word for "edge." Between June and September this area receives a small amount of rainfall, which is becoming less each year. The Sahel is highly susceptible to drought.

Most people of the Sahel are nomadic herders. They move the herds according to the rain and the growth of the grasses. Unfortunately, over-grazing, drought, deforestation, and overpopulation have damaged the fragile biome. The desert sand is continually covering the Sahel at an alarming rate.

Savanna

Tropical grasslands are flat, open plains scattered with shrubs and isolated trees. In Africa, they are called savannas. The temperature is warm year-round with a long dry season and a very wet season.

I just can't wait to be king.

The African savanna supports large herds of grazing animals. The most famous savanna is the Serengeti Plain which straddles the border between Kenya and Tanzania. Here, vast annual migrations of wildebeest and zebra can still be seen. Animals like lions, zebras, elephants, and giraffes graze or hunt. Many large herbivores–plant eating mammals–survive because they can move around and eat the plentiful grasses or graze on the Acacia trees. There are also lots of carnivores–meat eaters–that hunt the herbivores.

Survival on the savanna is closely linked to the seasons of drought and rain.

Internet Links: Fun 'drag and drop' map games at **Sheppard Software**. Play the Georegions game. Easylink to this site at **donnaward.net**

✏️ On your Biomes of Africa map, color the following regions a different color.
Desert (light brown)   Sahel (brown)   Rainforest (green)   Savanna (yellow)

Geographical Regions

Refer to an atlas and have on hand a copy of the *Topographical Map of Africa* from the Student Resources. Read a story or start a novel about Africa.

On the *Topographical Map of Africa* use a pencil and the help of an atlas to mark the following geographic regions.

Along the northeast coast of the continent, the **Atlas Mountains** stand guard next to the Sahara Desert. They stretch through Morocco, Algeria and Tunisia. Draw a pencil line on your Topographical Map to separate the Atlas Mountain Range from the Sahara Desert.

You will see on the map that the **Sahara Desert** is a combination of plains and rocky elevations. In fact, only one third of the Sahara Desert is sand. The borders of the Sahara Desert are the Atlantic Ocean in the west, the Atlas Mountains and Mediterranean Sea in the north, and the Red Sea in the east. Do not outline the Sahara Desert until reading further.

The **Great Rift Valley** in eastern Africa is the largest fault line in the earth's surface, running from Southeast Asia down into central Mozambique. The width of the valley may be from thirty to one hundred meters. It can be up to one kilometer or about half a mile deep and contains lakes and rivers. On the Topographical Map, you can see the mountains standing next to the desert, beginning at Eritrea on the Red Sea and along the border between Ethiopia and Sudan. Look on the map to see where the ridge divides into two, with Lake Victoria in between. Lake Malawi, also known as Lake Nyasa, forms the southern border of the Great Rift Valley, where the highlands join the South African Plateau. Use your atlas to identify these places and draw a line to show the outline of the Great Rift Valley.

The **South African Plateau** is a vast interior plain rimmed by rugged hills. The border along the top edge of the plateau runs along the northern national borders of Angola and Zambia. This rocky land holds a wealth of gold, diamonds, and other valuable minerals. Draw a line to show the north dividing edge of the South African Plateau.

In the center of the South Africa Plateau sits the **Kalahari Sand Basin** which contains the semi-arid Kalahari Desert. Draw a line around the Kalahari Sand Basin on your Topographical Map where the surface looks smooth.

The **Congo Basin** is the second largest river basin in the world, next to the Amazon. The waters from the surrounding areas all drain into tributaries of the Congo River which then flow into the Congo and eventually to the Atlantic Ocean. The Congo Basin straddles the equator and provides the ideal climate to sustain growth of the African Rainforest. The northern border of the Congo Basin runs halfway through Cameroon, into the Central African Republic and around the national border of the Democratic Republic of Congo. Draw a line on your map around the Congo Basin region.

Between the Sahara Desert and the Congo Basin, the transitional land of the **Sahel and Sudan** regions stretch across the bulge of Africa from the northern border of Senegal, through Mali, Niger, Chad, and Sudan to the edge of the Great Rift Valley. The Sudan region (not to be confused with the country, Sudan) is an area of savanna south of the Sahel. Draw a line from the north border of Senegal to Ethiopia to separate the Sahara Desert from the Sahel and Sudan regions.

The Topographical Map does not distinctly show the transition from desert to grassland. This division fluctuates annually with the rainfall; thus the Sahel and Sudan regions do not need to be separated.

Kalahari Desert

 Your map should now show the main geographical regions of Africa. Label these regions.

The Need for Water

Fill a bucket or water jug with as much water as you can carry. (4 litres/1 gallon weighs about 3.5 kg/8 lbs)
Go for a walk carrying the water 1–2 km/.5–1 mile if you can.

How much water does your family use? Where does the water come from before it reaches your taps? If you live in a rural area your water may come from a well. In towns and cities, water from lakes or other sources is purified at a treatment plant before it passes through pipelines to reach the homes. In the USA and Canada, the length of all the water pipes put together is enough to circle the earth 40 times! That is a lot of pipeline!

In developing countries many people do not have the luxury of running water in their homes. There may be a community tap, a well, or a river for water collection, or no source of water at all. Even if there is a water source, the water may be full of bacteria and unsafe for drinking.

Obtaining clean water is one of the primary concerns in many African communities. We simply turn on a tap, but an African child may spend several hours each day just collecting water for the family. This affects the child's ability to attend school. Children are often unhealthy from bacteria in the water. The following statistics show the seriousness of the problem.

- One in every six people lacks access to safe water.
- Ten million die each year from water-borne diseases
- Two million of those people are young children.
- There are 4 billion cases of diarrhea each year
- 2.5 million cases of diarrhea end in death.
- Every day about 6000 children die just from dehydration due to diarrhea.

Even in "water-rich" countries people should try to reduce excessive water use. Look at the chart of daily personal water use comparisons for various countries.

How much water do you think this African boy uses for his bath compared to what a child might use in your home?

Daily Personal Water Use Comparison
USA – 380 litres/100 gallons per person
Canada – 335 litres/88 gallons per person
Europe – 200 litres/53 gallons per person
Israel – 135 litres/35 gallons per person
Sub-Saharan Africa – 15 litres/4 gallons or less per person

Internet Links: Fun, interactive map games to learn the oceans and rivers at the **Sheppard Software** site. Easylink to this site at **donnaward.net**

'Lord, when did we ever see you hungry and feed you? Or thirsty and give you something to drink? Or a stranger and show you hospitality? Or naked and give you clothing?' And the King will say, 'I tell you the truth, when you did it to one of the least of these my brothers and sisters, you were doing it to me!'
Matthew 25:37-40

Using a blue pencil crayon, trace the rivers and lakes on your *Bodies of Water Map*. Label them with the help of an atlas.
View *Africa, a Land of Hope:* Episode 3–The Need for Water.

Use an atlas to help you label the oceans and bays on your Bodies of Water Map.

Solutions for the water problem in Africa are many and varied. The digging of wells is a common answer but is not suitable in every location. In volcanic mountainous regions the rocky ground is too hard to be penetrated. The people can collect only ground water. Often water is gathered from contaminated puddles, ditches and rivers causing serious health hazards. Swiss scientists have tested an inexpensive way for individuals to purify water for safe use. The **So**lar Water **Dis**infection (SODIS) process is simple and ideal for treating small quantities of water. Contaminated water is poured into transparent plastic bottles and exposed to sunlight for six hours. Micro organisms which cause disease are destroyed by sunlight through two methods:

1. Radiation within certain degrees of the equator.
2. Increased water temperature: if the water temperature rises above 50°C/122°F, the disinfection process is three times faster.

A retired Canadian chemist, Robert Dell, tested the process in the mountains of Uganda along the Rwandan border, where 1,800 Compassion sponsored children live. The hard volcanic soil eliminates the hope of digging wells and it is difficult to install latrines.

"On one of my first trips to Kisoro, Uganda, I had noticed that water collected by the children was polluted from land runoff through animal fecal matter. Dysentery and typhoid is epidemic. During a trip in 2003, I took testing equipment and measured the fecal E. coli count in drinking water in two rural areas where Compassion is working. The counts were alarmingly high and beyond any level of acceptability for drinking water.

We initiated the SODIS program with 24 families in March of 2004. Compassion had already been working to equip the town with rainwater storage tanks provided by a local manufacturer and the installation of pit latrines. We picked families that did not have rain catchment tanks and where there were known regular problems of diarrhea, dysentery, and typhoid in the homes. The Compassion staff began using the SODIS water process themselves thus giving confidence to the children.

Robert Dell and children of Kisoro.

After one year, severe diarrhea was eliminated (reduced from average incidents of 5 per week to 0 or 1). The improvement in the children's health was acknowledged by the parent(s) and by school teachers who commented on increased attendance and healthier, more alert students.

People in the community have seen the difference and are taking it upon themselves to start SODIS. Kisoro is only about 5 km/3 miles from the borders of Rwanda and the Democratic Republic of Congo. People in those countries have heard about it and are also initiating SODIS in their villages."[1]

SODIS has minimal cost and can be available to everyone. Even children can practice SODIS and remain healthy!

Twice a day, children as young as 6 or 7, many of them AIDS orphans, travel several kilometres to fetch water. They miss school and put themselves at risk of catching malaria to collect polluted water that causes intestinal diseases.

Internet Links: Go to the **SODIS** website for more stories about the success of SODIS. Easylink to this site at **donnaward.net**

1 Dell, Robert. SODIS Report. Used with permission.

View *Africa, a Land of Hope:* Episode 4–SODIS.

North Africa

Berber Proverb
(Algeria, Morocco)

Azru n-tmazirt yuf mraw n-wasif (Berber).

A stone from home is worth ten from the riverbed.

A girl from one's own village will know what is expected of her.
So a man is advised to marry a local girl rather than a stranger from the outside.
Everyone knows that a round boulder washed down by the stream will be useless for building, while
a slab cut from the cliff nearby will fit squarely into the wall. One stone at home is more
important than ten stones far away.

Resources

Internet:
Easylinks and updates for the following websites at donnaward.net

Affluenza. Find 100 ways to escape consumerism. A PBS site.
Africa, Explore the Regions. A PBS interactive site including geography, music, recipes and more.
AZ Arabian Camels. Unusual and interesting facts about the Arabian camel
Jim Miller's Images of Daily Life in Morocco.
National Geographic, The Nile Crocodile. Discover a unique reptile that is still fearsome on the Nile.
Odyssey World Trek. Young people travel around Africa bringing eyewitness accounts of people and places.

Books:
Berson, Harold. *Kassim's Shoes.* Humorous adaptation of a Moroccan folk tale (Ages 5-12).
De Bruycker, Daniel and Dauber, Maximilien. *Tintin's Travel Diaries, Egypt and the Middle East* (Ages 8-12).
Haldane, Elizabeth. *Desert.* 2006. A DK Book (All ages).
Kessler, Cristina. *One Night, A Story from the Desert.* A young Tuareg boy faces a desert night alone (Ages 5-12).
Jackson, Kay. *Explore the Desert* (Ages 8-12).
Raskin, Lawrie. *52 Days by Camel; My Sahara Adventure.* This is my favorite desert book (All ages).
Reynolds, Jan. *Sahara, Vanishing Culture.* Beautiful photos and information about the Tuareg (All ages).
Look in your library adult section for photo books. DDC - 916.6

Films:
National Geographic Africa: Episode 2–Desert Odyssey. A nine-year old boy embarks on his first camel
    caravan to make a 1,500-mile, six-month trek. Highly recommended.
Lawrence of Arabia. Made in Arabia but shows desert life of the Bedouin.
Beau Geste. This 1939 classic tale of three English brothers who join the French Foreign Legion and experience
    army life in the desert. See review and summary at **Greatest Films**.
Mystery of the Nile (IMAX film) See the **Mystery of the Nile** website.

News Notes:
After the collapse of France's African empire in the '50s and '60s, many North Africans from countries like Libya and Algeria emigrated to France in search of employment. Second and third generation immigrants who felt marginalized in French society instigated the Paris Riots of 2005. Go to Easylinks at **donnaward.net** for news links about this event.

Photograph previous page: The parc de la Ligue Arabe in Casablanca, Morocco

Read *52 Days by Camel*, or look at photos of North Africa.

The Sahara Desert lurks with endless severity beyond the pleasant coastal lowlands of North Africa. For centuries, outsiders have been fascinated with the mystique of this wasteland, the world's largest, hottest desert. It covers almost one-quarter of the continent of Africa and serves as the border between the Arab-influenced north and the black-African south. Sahara simply means "desert" in Arabic.

Along with vast basins of sand and huge shifting dunes, the Sahara Desert also contains mountains, rocky outcrops, and large gravel plains. Two rivers, the Nile in the east and the Niger of the southwest, support most of the people who live in the desert area. In a few locations, water from an underground river seeps to the surface and allows plants to grow in an exotic oasis completely surrounded by sand. At the largest oases, towns have grown up.

The climate of the desert is extremely hot and dry; however, a few mountain peaks have snow at the top for parts of the year. The winds are unpredictable, blowing sometimes for days, changing the shapes of the dunes and reducing visibility to zero. Powerful sandstorms can be extremely unpleasant and dangerous for anyone caught in them.

The Nile Valley is a narrow strip of fertile land sandwiched on each side by desert. On a map, trace the route of the Nile with your finger. At 6,695 km/4,160 miles, it is the longest river in the world. The Nile is made up of two rivers, the White Nile flowing from Lake Victoria, and the smaller Blue Nile which flows from Lake Tana in Ethiopia. See if you can find where these rivers join in the country of Sudan to continue the long journey north.

In Egypt, the Nile spreads out into one of the world's largest river deltas, its tributaries covering 240 km/150 miles of the Mediterranean coastline as it drains into the sea. The delta provides very rich farmland in stark contrast to the desert just beyond.

There is scant rainfall in Egypt, but heavy spring rains at the source of the Nile swell the water volume each summer. Prior to the building of the Aswan Dam to control the water flow, the delta would flood every year. When the water receded it left behind fertile soil for crops where there would otherwise be desert.

This photograph from space shows the green farmland of the Nile Delta against the desert surrounding it. The Red Sea separates the Sinai Peninsula from the rest of Egypt. Note the Suez Canal extending to the Mediterranean Sea from the Red Sea.

Write the names of the following countries and their capital cities on your *Political Map Of Africa*:
Algeria, Morocco, Egypt, Tunisia, Libya, Western Sahara.

Living in the Maghreb

📖 Look at resources about Morocco or another country of the Maghreb.

Three distinct cultural regions naturally divide the people groups of North Africa: the Maghreb region along the northwest coast, the Sahara Desert, and the Nile Valley of Egypt.

The countries of North Africa are Muslim nations. The people feel more closely linked with nations of the Middle East than they do with the rest of Africa. The first people were Berbers and when the Arabs invaded in the 6th century, Islam became the dominant religion. Mass Arab migration in later years strengthened the Arab culture in such a way that the distinction between Berbers and Arabs is sometimes non-existent.

Berber warriors at a show in Morocco

The Maghreb is the cultural region north of the Sahara Desert and west of the Nile River. It includes the coastal area of Morocco, Western Sahara, Algeria, Tunisia, and Libya. In Arabic, Maghreb simply means 'western.'

Morocco has a strategic location along the Strait of Gibraltar, which is the doorway to the Mediterranean Sea. Only 14 km/8.5 miles separates Europe from Africa at the narrowest point. Illegal immigrants who hope to find a better life in Europe usually enter Europe from Morocco.

The Barbary Coast, or Barbary, was the term used by Europeans until the 19th century to refer to the coastal regions of the Maghreb. This term came from the Greek word *barbaros*, which means 'the sound foreigners make.' The name became associated with Arab slave traders and the Barbary pirates who lived on the North African coast. The pirates attacked ships traveling in the Mediterranean Sea and the Atlantic Ocean.

In colonial times, when European powers ruled most of Africa, France controlled the countries of Morocco, Algeria, and Tunisia. While Arabic is the official language of these countries, French is the language of business. Libya was under Italian rule until independence in 1951. It was the first African country to achieve freedom under the direction of the United Nations. In the 1970's, Morocco took control of Western Sahara. This is an area still in dispute.

Almond Milk (Morocco)
3/4 cup toasted almonds, finely ground in a coffee grinder
1/2 cup firmly packed brown sugar
1 cup water   4 cups milk
1 tablespoon orange zest—grated orange peel.
(Avoid the white pith as it is bitter.)
In a bowl, combine the almonds and the sugar. Add 1/2 cup of water and let soak for 30 minutes. Put in a blender and blend on low speed as you drizzle in the remaining water. Blend well and let stand for 30 minutes.
Slightly warm the milk and stir in the orange zest. Pour the almond mixture into the milk and pass through a fine mesh sieve. Stir well and serve, or serve when chilled.

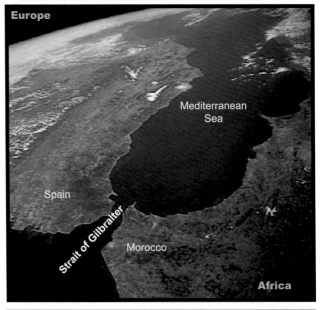

Europe
Mediterranean Sea
Spain
Strait of Gilbralter
Morocco
Africa

Internet Links: Easylink to photo sites at **donnaward.net**

 Complete a *Country Fact* notebook page about Morocco.

Living in the Desert

📖 Look at a resource about the Tuareg people or desert travel.

In the Sahara there is a clear difference between the settled Berbers who live in permanent villages beside oases, and the semi nomadic Berbers, predominantly the Tuareg, who travel seasonally in search of pasture.

Bahariya Oasis - Egypt

The Tuareg have been camel breeders and caravan leaders for centuries. The Tuareg men are called the Blue Men, because they conceal their faces up to the eyes with a veil of indigo blue, which leaves a blue stain on their skin. The cloth is believed to ward off evil spirits, but it also provides protection against harsh desert sands.

For over a thousand years, the Tuareg controlled the trans-Saharan caravan trade that brought gold and slaves from southern Africa to the coastal ports, and salt from within the Sahara itself. The camels would be fattened on the grasses of the Sahel for several months and then assembled into a caravan. The caravan faced dangers from bandits, sandstorms, and lack of water. Only great skill ensured survival. Advanced runners were sent to an oasis to send water back to the caravan when it was still several days away, as not enough water could be carried to make the full journey.

The Tuareg today still lead caravans across the desert to the salt mines. Tuareg women grow crops in their seasonal villages. Many Tuareg are trying to adapt to modern urban life as drought and lack of trading opportunities make it difficult to continue the traditional lifestyle.

Desertification

Settled regions around the Sahara Desert are always under the threat of desertification. The Sahel is shrinking every year. This process happens as sand encroaches on fertile soil and more and more land becomes desert. People damage the terrain by cutting too many trees for fire wood, allowing animals to over graze, or by planting the same crops repeatedly until the soil is worn out. Desertification threatens desert towns and pasture land.

Living in two worlds. Traditional ways—new technology. Cher stays in touch on a satellite phone (below).

Internet Links: Listen to Tuareg music, try some Tuareg recipes and read more about these people at **PBS Africa: Explore the Regions** web site. Easylink to this site and others about the Sahara people at **donnaward.net**

✏️ View *National Geographic Africa*: Episode 2–Desert Odyssey or look at a resource with photos of the people of the desert.
Complete a *Facts About People* notebook page about the Tuareg people.

Living in the Nile Valley

📖 Look at a resource or photographs of Egypt.

The People of the Nile have flourished along the banks of this great river since ancient times. The abundant food allowed Egyptian culture to thrive. When the summer floods were at their highest and the farmers could not work the land, they were conscripted to build Pyramids as tombs for their kings. These monuments can still be seen along the Nile River.

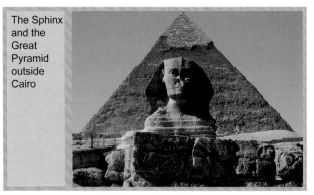
The Sphinx and the Great Pyramid outside Cairo

In modern times, as the population along the river grew, it became necessary to control the flood waters to protect farmland. The Aswan High Dam was built in 1960 to prevent flooding, generate electricity, and provide water for agriculture. Damage from flooding is now eliminated, however, the dam has produced new problems for farmers. They now have to dump tons of artificial fertilizer on the land to make up for the lack of fresh soil from the floods.

Erosion along the delta coastal area means that soil is falling into the sea but is no longer being replaced by new river sediment. Much of the delta farmland is now considered poor quality for farming.

The river is still used as a transportation route. Nile cruises are a popular tourist attraction, as most of the sites to see are along the Nile.

The Suez Canal is a strategic shipping lane which allows for significantly shorter routes between Europe and Asia. The canal was completed in 1869. On a map of the world trace the course a ship would have to take from India to Europe without the Suez Canal. You can see why this canal is so important.

Twice in the history of the canal it has been closed because of international conflict. In the Suez Crisis of 1956, the Egyptian President took control of the canal causing Britain, France, and Israel to invade Egypt. The United Nations sent troops to prevent war until a peace agreement could be negotiated. The canal was closed until the following year while it was being cleared of sunken ships and land mines.

Again in 1967, when Egypt was defeated by Israel in the Six-Day War, the canal was closed. It did not open again until 1975 at the conclusion of the Yom Kippur War.

Today, the canal is open to ships of every nation. Over 25,000 ships use the canal annually. The photograph shows how the desert stretches right to the banks of the canal.

Easylinks to photo and **World Trek in Egypt** at **donnaward.net**

✏️ Complete a *Country Facts* notebook page about Egypt.

Camels and Crocodiles

📖 Look at resources about camels and/or crocodiles.

The Nile crocodile lives south of the Aswan High Dam and throughout Africa. It is an unusual reptile. Most reptiles do not watch over their young, but the Nile crocodile guards her nest full of eggs for three months until the young crocs hatch. Then she will carry the babies in her mouth to the water and care for them for up to two years. Nile crocodiles will eat almost anything from small fish to large mammals such as giraffes or antelope. They are dangerous to humans.

Can you see the camel's long, beautiful eyelashes? And look! It can close its nose. Can you do that? The camel's double eye-lashes and strong nose muscles are there for a reason. When the wind whips the sand around, the camel can protect itself from the stinging blasts.

Camels are uniquely built for desert journeys. They can travel for up to seven days without food or water. Their hump stores fatty tissue which gives energy to the body. The camel has unique blood cells which can absorb water more quickly than other creatures, and store it for a long time in the blood stream. A camel can drink up to 100 litres/21 gallons in ten minutes, a feat which would kill other animals. Camels can withstand intense heat without sweating which helps them conserve water.

Wide, padded feet help the camel not to sink into the sand especially when carrying a heavy load. Camels are nicknamed "ships of the desert" because they walk like the motion of a rolling boat–moving both feet on one side, and then both feet on the other.

Camels have been known to be bad-tempered, spitting when angered. They bawl and moan when rising to their feet with a load, like the groans of a weightlifter hoisting a heavy burden. Camels can carry up to 495kg/990lb, however, 165kg/330lb is the most comfortable load for a camel to carry. No animal is suited to desert travel as superbly as the camel.

The Crocodile Song (Traditional campfire song)
Oh she sailed away
On a sunny, summer day
On the back of a crocodile.
(Put palm on back of other hand, rotate thumbs as oars).
"So you see," said she,
"He's as tame as he can be,
I'll ride him down the Nile."
(Pat back of hand as you would a pet).
Well, the croc winked his eye (point to wink),
As she waved them all good-bye (wave),
Wearing a happy smile (trace smile on face).
At the end of the ride,
The lady was inside (rub tummy).
And the smile was on the crocodile. (Trace smile).

Internet Links: Find out unusual facts in **AZ of Arabian Camels** site or visit **National Geographic** to read about the Nile Crocodile. Easylink to these sites at **donnaward.net**

 Complete an *Animal Facts* notebook page about the camel or the crocodile.

Managing Affluence with Integrity

How big is your house? Many homes in the slums of Africa are no bigger than one of your smallest bedrooms.

In Kenya, George is very excited to receive a ball from his visiting sponsor. The children in his neighborhood kick around stones instead of balls. When their basic needs of food, shelter, and clothing are met, these children are happy with simple games and a few toys. Contrast this with the children of affluent families who are surrounded by expensive toys but frequently complain of boredom. Do you or your friends ever feel bored? Take a look at all your belongings. How many play things do you own and how often do you use them? Could you be happy with less?

The more people fill their lives with things, the more they tell psychiatrists or pastors that they feel "empty" inside. Two thousand years ago, Jesus Christ predicted they would feel that way. "What profit would it bring a person," He asked his followers "were that person to gain the whole world, but lose his soul?" (Matt. 16:26).

When asked, "What is enough?" a rich man replied,
"Just a little bit more."

Presently, people in North America are earning much higher salaries than their parents did. They are spending more and saving less. In 1980, people put about 10 percent of their salary into savings. In 1996, it was reported that North Americans were saving about 4 percent of their earnings. By the year 2000, the savings rate hovered around zero. Meanwhile, impoverished Chinese, Indian, and Pakistani workers save a quarter of their incomes. [1]

When more goods are purchased, additional care and maintenance is required to keep everything working. If a family moves to a bigger house, it involves more cleaning. Sports equipment needs repairs. Computers need anti-spam, pop-up blockers, updated programs and defragging. It all adds up to keeping everyone too busy. When we buy things to make our lives better, it often makes life more complicated instead.

Swelling expectations lead to a constant effort to keep up with the latest products. That, in turn, forces us to work more, so we can afford the goods we desire. With so many items to purchase and the need to work harder to obtain them, our lives grow more harried and pressured. What do you think the following comment says about this problem?

Even if you win the rat race, you're still a rat.

People don't need enormous cars, they need respect. They don't need closets full of clothes, they need to feel attractive and they need excitement and variety and beauty. People don't need electronic equipment; they need something worthwhile to do with their lives. People need identity, community, challenge, acknowledgement, love, and joy. To try to fill these needs with material things is to set up an unquenchable appetite for false solutions to real and never-satisfied problems. The resulting psychological emptiness is one of the major forces behind the desire for material growth. [2]

Jesus said, "Beware! Guard against every kind of greed. Life is not measured by how much you own." Luke 12:15

Internet Links: Visit the PBS site about **Affluenza** to find 100 ways to escape consumerism and over spending. Easylink to this site at **donnaward.net**

1 De Graaf, John; Wann, David; Naylor, Thomas; Simon, Scott. *Affluenza: The All Consuming Epidemic.* 2001, p. 2.
2 Meadows, Dennis and Donella; Randers, Jorgen. *Beyond the Limits.* 1992, p. 111.

View *Africa, A Land of Hope*: Episode 4–Jackie. How is her life different than yours in areas such as school, chores, and everyday living?

West Africa

Dagbani Proverb
(Ghana)

Naawuni yi kabigi a gbali, o ni wuhi a ni yen kpahi shem (Dagbani).

If God breaks your leg, He will teach you how to limp.

It is not unusual for people to suffer misfortunes in terms of sickness, accidents or other mishaps. We will all suffer many difficulties in our lives. A farmer may work hard all during the rainy season on his rice farm. The rains may also be plentiful. The rice germinates and produces abundantly. Then a few days before he is to harvest the rice, someone burns some brush in a nearby farm; the fire gets out of control and burns most of his rice field. The farmer does not despair. He harvests the remaining rice and knows that God will still provide for him. So if God allows troubles or sufferings, He will also show us how to manage quite well in spite of them.

Resources

Internet:
Easylinks and updates for the following websites at donnaward.net

Africa, Explore the Regions. Visit the Sahel and the Rainforest on this PBS site.
Niger Currents, Introduction. Two Canadians with *Engineers Without Borders* travel the Niger River.
National Public Radio. Advanced Listeners can listen to the 7 part series *Oil Money Divides Nigeria* about the
   Niger River Delta.
All Africa. Search by topic for current events such as the Niger Delta Conflict and more.
Odyssey World Trek. Visit Mali and West Africa with the trekkers.

Books:
Diakité, Penda. *I Lost My Tooth in Africa.* A true story from Mali (Ages 5-10).
George, Michael. *Deserts.* Images Series. Fascinating full colour photos with short text (All ages).
George, Michael. *Rain Forest.* Images Series that combines stunning photos with text (All ages).
Granfield, Linda. *Amazing Grace.* John Newton and the slave trade (All ages).
Masoff , Joy. *Mali: Land of Gold & Glory.* Colour, living book. Timbuktu & the Mali Kingdom (Ages 8-12).
Watson, Pete. *The Heart of the Lion.* An American boy journals the culture of West Africa (Ages 5-12).

African Folktales:
Aardema, Verna. *Anansi does the Impossible.* Anansi the Spider is the hero of Ashanti tales of West Africa (Ages 5-12).
Aardema, Verna. *Anansi finds a fool : an Ashanti tale* (Ages 5-12).
Aardema, Verna. *Koi And The Kola Nuts : A Tale From Liberia* (Ages 5-12).
Aardema, Verna. *Oh, Kojo! How Could You!: An Ashanti Tale* (Ages 5-12).
Aardema, Verna. *Princess Gorilla And A New Kind Of Water: A Mpongwe Tale* (Ages 5-12).
Aardema, Verna. *The Vingananee And The Tree Toad : A Liberian Tale* (Ages 5-12).
Aardema, Verna. *Why Mosquitoes Buzz In People's Ears : A West African Tale* (Ages 5-12).
Courlander, Harold and Herzog, George. *The Cow-Tail Switch and Other West African Stories.* (Ages 8-12).
Mandela, Nelson (ed). *Nelson Mandela's Favorite African Folktales* (All ages).
Washington, Donna L. *A Pride of African Tales.* Six African stories with beautiful illustrations (Ages 8-14).
Watson, Pete. *The Market Lady and the Mango Tree* (Ages 5-12).

Films:
National Geographic Africa: Episode 5–Love in the Sahel.

Photograph previous page: The beach at Cape Coast, Ghana.

Look at photos of West Africa or explore a website such as Odyssey World Trek.

If you were traveling to West Africa, what would you put in your suitcase? It would depend on where you were going. West African climate and vegetation varies dramatically from the dry desert in the north to the sparse arid grassland of the Sahel, and finally to portions of tropical rainforest along the coast (although most of it has disappeared because of logging and urbanization).

Would you like to travel by camel in the Saharan part of West Africa? Maybe you will go to see Timbuktu, one of the most popular tourist attractions. Or maybe you will go to Niger, one of the hottest countries in the world, where it is constantly dry and dusty. You had better bring along a cotton scarf to keep the sand from blowing in your eyes and nose.

Niger takes its name from the Niger River, which winds on a very unusual route. Rivers flow towards the sea; but the Niger's current sends it away from the sea and into the desert instead. Look on a map to see how close the source of the Niger is to the Atlantic Ocean. Its route takes it northeast, away from the ocean, and then it makes a sharp right turn southeast toward the Gulf of Guinea. The bend, which is the closest major water source to the desert, is the location of Timbuktu. This mysterious river route baffled European geographers for centuries.

If you are going to travel to the coast, go between December and May, when it is warm and dry. In the rainy season you are likely to get caught in a monsoonal-type downpour or maybe even a flood. Countries along the coast experience torrential rains, flooding, and hot, humid weather between May and November. Sierra Leone sees the most rainfall of the West African countries with up to 495 cm/195 inches a year. Measure it. That is a lot of rain!

The coastline varies from lagoons and mangrove swamps, such as in Liberia, to the heavy rolling surf and sand of Ivory Coast, known officially by its French name, Côte d'Ivoire. Ghana contains the largest reservoir in the world, Lake Volta, and the dam which holds it back provides most of the electricity for Ghana and the surrounding countries.

The Niger River Delta in Nigeria is one of the largest deltas in Africa, next to the Nile. Some tributaries are clogged with sand bars, and there are mangrove swamps. There are other channels deep enough for ocean vessels to navigate. You can probably pick those out on the photo below. The delta is a densely populated but poverty-stricken area.

There are rich oilfields in the delta, but they are controlled by the government and international companies. Residents are outraged to live in poverty with no share of the profit. Militant groups have attacked the oil companies by taking their workers hostage. Armed clashes between the Nigerian military and rebel groups make this area very unstable and oil production is seriously hampered. After many years of rule by a dictator, Nigeria now has a democratic government. There is hope for improvement, but it will take time.

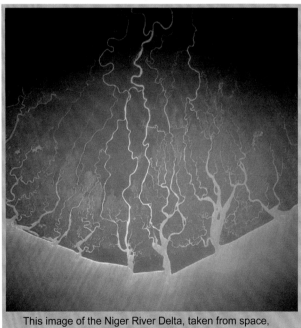

This image of the Niger River Delta, taken from space, shows the great expanse of its many tributaries.

Use an atlas to write the names of the following countries (with capital cities) on your political map: Benin, Burkina Faso, Cape Verde, Chad, Côte d'Ivoire, Gambia, Ghana, Guinea Bissau, Liberia, Mali, Mauritania, Niger, Senegal, Sierra Leone, Togo.

Ancient Kingdoms of West Africa

 Read *Mali: Land of Gold & Glory* or another book about ancient West African kingdoms.
Read *Exploring Africa* pp. 8, 24, 26 or another book about exploration.

Ancient Empires

Gold! Ivory! Great schools of learning! The rich cities of Timbuktu and Djenne flourished once at the base of the Saharan caravan route, on the bend of the Niger River. In 1240, Sundiata Keita was building strong links between the trading caravans of the north and his Mali Empire at the southern edge of the Sahara.

The Mali kingdom was conquered around 1500 by the Songhay Empire which also grew rich with the gold trade. After Moroccan raiders overthrew the Songhay Empire in 1591, the territory was governed by smaller powers and city states, while Portuguese, French, and English traders began building their slave trading forts along the coast.

An explorer, willing to travel the long, arduous road to Timbuktu, would likely be killed there by the Muslim residents who were hostile to outsiders. The city was fabled to be built of gold and reaching it became the obsession of many Europeans, to their peril! The name "Timbuktu" became synonymous with any unreachable place and is still a term used today. If you asked someone, "Can you come to Hawaii?" the reply, "That's like going to Timbuktu!" would mean that it is impossible.

The historical worth of Timbuktu caused it to be named a World Heritage Site in 1988 and, as such, it will be protected from decay. This once flourishing city is now a desert town, poor, unimpressive except in legend, and always in danger of desertification. Tourism keeps the city alive.

Sign: Timbuktu 52 Days by Camel

Ibn Battuta (1304-1377)

At only 21 years old, the Muslim explorer, Ibn Battuta, left Morocco for twenty-three years of travel through the Middle East, India, China, and the coast of East Africa before returning home. He left again, in 1349, to travel through Northern Africa. He crossed the Sahara with a caravan heading to trade in the south. He passed through Timbuktu and sailed down the Niger River, which he thought flowed west. When he returned home five years later, Battuta wrote a book of his travels entitled *Rihla*.

René Caillié (1799-1838)

At 16, René Caillié of France traveled to West Africa intending to explore the interior. Eleven years later, disguised as a Muslim, Caillié was the first European to visit legendary Timbuktu and survive to tell the tale. Imagine his disappointment when he found a city made of mud instead of gold. At risk of death, he stayed two weeks making notes. Then he joined a 1,200 camel caravan for the torturous trek across the Sahara. It took another six weeks to traverse the Atlas Mountains and finally sail home to France. His story was doubted until Heinrich Barth confirmed Caillié's findings.

Heinrich Barth (1821-1865)

Heinrich Barth was a German working for the British government. He traveled from Tunisia across the Sahara to Timbuktu and back across the Sahara again in spite of many dangers and difficulties. His companions died on the journey. He was able to confirm Caillié's claims.

 View *National Geographic Africa*: Episode 5–Love in the Sahel. Complete a *Country Facts* notebook page about Mali.

Slavery to Independence

📖 Read *Exploring Africa*, p. 18; *The Africans* or another book about the Slave Trade.

Atiku woke in alarm! Did he hear voices? He sat up for awhile but only heard the crickets singing through the night. Every night Atiku slept in fear that the people stealers would come to tear apart families, burn villages, and take captive the young and strong. Slavery had been practised for centuries in Africa, but when

the Europeans became involved, powerful African nations exchanged slaves for firearms, and the slave trade began in earnest. Young men like Atiku were captured and herded to the coast where traders packed them mercilessly into ships bound for America.

In the new European colonies in North and South America there was a shortage of labor, and slavery was the chosen solution. The first African slaves arrived in Hispaniola (Haiti and Dominican Republic) in 1502 and the trade continued until finally, in 1853, Brazil became the last nation to disband and outlaw the slave trade. In 351 years, it is estimated that over 30 million Africans were captured but only one of every three made it to the New World alive.

The descendents of these slaves, now living around the world, are recognized as still having an integral part in the development of Africa and are called the African Diaspora.

Just as the slave trade was being abolished, the European powers were scrambling for control of Africa. The advantage of firearms helped to crush any native resistance. During the Colonial Period, France and England held most of the power in West Africa. Ghana achieved independence in 1957, followed shortly by the rest of West Africa.

Since attaining independence, civil war and corruption has hampered growth, especially in countries with a wealth of natural resources. For years the sale of smuggled diamonds funded the civil war in Sierre Leone. Nigeria's oil reserves cause disputes. Liberia and Côte d'Ivoire are other countries greatly affected by long-standing civil hostilities.

Ellen Johnson-Sirleaf

In 2005, in a peaceful and democratic election, Liberia voters elected Ellen Johnson-Sirleaf as their president. She is the first female head of state in African history, and the first female black president in the world. Her strong will and resolve in the face of difficulty has earned her the nickname "Iron Lady."

In 1792, Freetown in Sierre Leone was established as a haven for freed slaves. Coming from all parts of Africa, the people were united by their common experience of slavery.

Internet Links: Visit the BBC site to explore Slavery in **A Story of Africa.** See news video as a reporter accompanies the U.N. on a disarming mission in Liberia at **Frontline World Liberia.** Easylink at **donnaward.net**

> Anyone who says something small can't make a difference, has never been in bed with a mosquito.
> Anonymous.

✏️ Complete a *Country Facts* notebook page about Liberia, or a *Facts About People* page on Ellen Johnson-Sirleaf.

Missionaries and Explorers

📖 Read *Exploring Africa*, p. 22, or a similar book.

Samuel Ajayi Crowther, born in 1807 in Western Africa, grew up in dangerous times, when the threat of slave traders was constant. When Ajayi was thirteen, his village was raided and he faced the horror of capture and being torn from his family. Before going far, the slave ship on which Ajayi was imprisoned was intercepted and the slaves were rescued by the British navy and put ashore in Freetown, Sierra Leone.

It was here that Ajayi became a committed Christian. He recorded that he thus escaped a worse state of slavery, namely, slavery to sin. Ajayi became a schoolmaster for other liberated slaves and began learning one after another, the many languages spoken by the freed Africans. He began traveling up the Niger River with the gospel message of peace. One memorable excursion took him to his native Nigeria, where he was reunited with his mother and sister after twenty long years of separation.

In 1864, Crowther was ordained as the first African bishop of the Anglican Church of England. The Yoruba language became the initial African language to be used in Anglican worship. He was one of the first graduates from sub-Saharan Africa's only university at the time, which was built on the site of an old Arab slave market.

Crowther's dynamic ministry was effective in opposing slavery, witchcraft, and Islam. He was successful in giving Africans an Evangelical Anglicanism which was truly African. Today there are 18 times more Anglicans worshipping in church every Sunday in Nigeria than there are in Great Britain.

African Explorers in Africa

African people traveled in Africa for three predominant reasons. The first was when war or famine threatened the safety of a group of people, and they made the dangerous trek to relocate. Commerce was the second reason as merchants traveled to trade in salt, gold, slaves, or cloth. Finally, religious interests caused Muslims and Christians to travel to spread their faith or make pilgrimages. A few Muslim explorers from North Africa also journeyed just to learn of new places and people.

Mungo Park (1771-1806)
This tenacious Scottish explorer drowned while exploring the Niger River.

European Explorers in Africa

European interests were similar to those of African explorers. The first European travelers to Africa traded along the coastlines with Africans who brought slaves or goods to the ports. Later, Christian missionaries came to win converts. Finally, like some Muslim travelers, Europeans wanted to explore places new to them. In the 19th century, European geographers were consumed with discovering the source of the two great rivers, the Niger and the Nile.

A Truly African Game

Oware is an ancient game originating in Africa and is the official game of Ghana. It is found in great variety across the continent. In East Africa it is called Mancala. In South Africa it is called Ohoro.

Pit and pebble games are probably the oldest family of games and have been used both by merchants in calculating sums, and by all ages as an enjoyable pastime. In its simplest form, Oware can be played by scooping holes in the dirt and using seeds or pebbles as counters. The game can be introduced as an easy game of chance to very young children, but can become a complicated strategy/mathematical game played by serious adults.

Internet Links: Go to **The Oware Society** for rules on how to play. Easylink to this site at **donnaward.net**

 Make an Oware game with an egg carton and seeds or pebbles, or complete a *Facts About People* notebook page for an explorer or missionary.

Simple Living with Style

Discuss what events and activities cause your family stress in the week. Talk about helpful things each person can do to make things run smoothly.

"Everything I always wanted, I got! I bought a ski chalet in the mountains and a beach resort in the Pacific. I purchased a villa in France, with vineyards and gardeners, and a French chef — fabulous! There were treasures and toys, servants and food. I denied myself nothing. I became greater by far than anyone around. I enjoyed it all, but as I looked over all that I had toiled to achieve, the realization came that all of it was meaningless, like chasing the wind" (Adaptation of Ecclesiastes 2).

King Solomon, the wisest man who ever lived (and likely the richest), discovered that there is an emptiness to having great wealth. People in the developed world are working, working, working – they can never keep up with all the things they want to buy and achieve. Suddenly, they realize that they don't have time for family and friends. Life is chaotic. The rat race is exhausting! Everything has a cost. What do you think people lose when they predominantly strive after wealth?

David Thoreau, a famous American author wrote in 1854, "Our life is frittered away by detail. . . Simplify, simplify."

The Quakers "Testimony of Simplicity" is the belief that a person should live simply so as to focus on what is really important and ignore what is least important. The inner condition is considered more important than the outward appearance. The value of spiritual life and character should far outweigh possessions. They believe, as should we all, that our resources, such as money and time, should be deliberately used to make life truly better for oneself and others.

Frugal simplicity is an attempt to manage money carefully and buy less. How much "stuff" do you have in your home that you could live without? If you were going to "dejunk" your room, how many things could you throw out or give away? When we "reduce, reuse, and recycle" we are making an effort to reduce garbage and stuff around our homes, and save valuable resources such as water and energy which are used to make the products.

Minimize overspending by becoming an advertising critic. Advertisements are meant to convince people to buy, buy, buy! Don't be fooled! Try the method of one family, who required the children when they were watching television, to shout after each advertisement, "Who do you think you're kidding?" Become cynical about advertising.

An African saying: *Mzungas* (white people) have the watches but Africans have the time, all the time in the world.

Uncluttered simplicity is the effort to simplify schedules. Those in wealthy societies often find their lives too busy and too stressed. Uncluttered simplicity means trying to step out of the hectic lifestyle to eliminate trivial distractions and focus on the essentials. They will be different for each unique life and family.

Jesus spoke about both the distractions of life and greed when he told a parable about the seed that fell on thorny ground. He said, "The one who received the seed that fell among the thorns is the man who hears the word (of God), but the worries of this life and the deceitfulness of wealth choke it, making it unfruitful." What do the thorns represent?

Choosing to simplify your life means keeping your priorities on the things that really matter, instead of becoming caught in materialism. Education and good jobs are very important, as long as your work and earning power stays in perspective. Keep your life rich with family, friends, community, creative work, and a spiritual connection.

View *Africa, A Land of Hope:* Episode 5–Legacy of Dreams Fulfilled.

Live and Die by the Sling

The following are excerpts from *Too Small to Ignore, Why Children are the Next Big Thing*, by Dr. Wess Stafford, President & CEO of Compassion International. He was the son of missionaries to West Africa.

I began wrapping my left thumb and forefinger around the two prongs of the slingshot the way I knew would guarantee steadiness. I picked a shiny marble out of the jar. This was going to be even easier than I thought. Unlike the irregular stones we had to use in the village, that required an extra calculation before firing, these totally smooth and perfectly round marbles would fly straight and true. I raised the slingshot, pulled back the rubber, and with one flashing flick of my wrist, splink! Went a bottle on the far end. A shower of glass exploded in all directions. The man stared at me while brushing bits of glass from his hair and clothing.

"Whoa, beginner's luck, huh?" he growled.

"Well, maybe not," I replied as I picked up another marble. Blam! Down went the second bottle. A crowd was beginning to grow behind me.

"I'm guessin' you've done this before," the man hissed.

"Well, yeah, we do this where I come from," I answered. With that, I picked up my third marble and pulverized the third bottle. The crowd cheered. The man winced.

Success – my first in America! My village buddies would have doubled over with laughter at my having won such a huge victory with so little challenge.

My mind wandered five thousand miles across the Atlantic to my little village of Nielle (Ivory Coast). The hot, dusty town was five hundred miles inland, about as far as anyone dared venture on the washboard – riddled path we called a road. I knew that by now the corn and millet would be tall and ripening in the fields surrounding the village. Now the harvest was approaching, and the rewards for the hard work could almost be tasted. It was time to send in the boys and their trusty slings! Every plant was precious, and our very lives depended on bringing an adequate harvest into the little thatched-roof mud silos beside our huts. We loved this time of year because it allowed us boys to protect the harvest from marauding troops of baboons and monkeys that could destroy an unguarded field in a single night. This was dangerous work, since a full-grown, fanged male baboon can weigh more than fifty pounds. In large troops, baboons fear almost nothing, certainly not a little boy – unless he is lethally armed and skilled!

Perched on our stilted posts, we stood watch until the corn was harvested. We often just sent warning shots at the rustling sounds in the elephant grass. If a big baboon still dared to trespass into our field, he was met with a hailstorm of rocks. If a troop of thirty baboons invaded, we took no prisoners. Any baboon we killed became instant lunch.

When my mother told us boys about the Bible epic of David killing Goliath with a sling, we merely shrugged. I remember thinking, That was one stupid giant. I could have done that myself! Great big forehead, stationary giant just a few feet away – no problem! The bit about David choosing five smooth stones from the stream made perfect sense to my little band of marksmen. When you live and die by the sling as we did, you're always walking around with one eye on the ground looking for the next perfect stone. Round rocks are hard to come by and can make all the difference in the world. If one has a little bump on a side, the rock can veer off in flight. I'm pretty sure David picked up five smooth stones simply because there they were right in front of him. All us boys knew he should need only one to take care of Goliath, but why pass up the other four?

When it came to herding cattle, we had to keep them from wandering off by landing a well-aimed rock along their flanks from time to time. To these leathery behemoths, it probably felt like a tsetse fly sting. We laughed that they probably said to one another, "Did you ever notice how nasty the flies bite when those little boys come around?" A herd of fifty huge Brahman cattle could be managed by no more than two little boys with slingshots.

When we weren't firing at animals, we used our slings for picking mangoes. Mango trees tend to be infested with swarms of nasty, stinging red ants. To try to shinny up a mango tree was to announce to the world, "I am a complete idiot and don't know any better." So we boys would target the long slender stem by which each fruit hung. We would zing a rock up there and cleanly clip the stem. Our buddies would catch the falling mango – or get hit by it, which was even better. We took the challenge up a notch by aiming at the mango stem *while jogging* past the tree.

Now on the Coney Island midway, I pointed. "Okay, I'll have that big bear with the black nose, way up there!"

"Not so fast!" the barker sneered. With a sarcastic flare, he pulled out a fuzzy little bear about four inches tall.

Fine. I had seen this kind of trickery among the Dyoula craftsmen down the road. I plunked down another quarter. Pow, pow, pow. Three more bottles shattered.

"Okay, now I want that big one," I announced with a slight edge in my voice.

Reality set in. The guy could see a pattern developing. This skinny little kid was going to shatter all his pop bottles. He got out his stick and unhooked my teddy bear – the huge brown one with the black nose. "Look, kid, just take this miserable bear and get outta my face!" he snapped.

I smiled as I walked away with my prize. The crowd was silent for a moment as they relished the drama that had just played out in front of them. Good had triumphed over evil. They broke out in wild cheers and applause.

Central Africa

Tembo Proverb
(Democratic Republic of Congo)

Keshi walyire kataera (Tembo).

A debt is not a loss once one knows the debtor.

Debt is one of the forms of sharing, of putting goods to the disposal of the community.
We say that the one who lends to you is the one who values you and puts his confidence in you.
The one who gives out his goods to his fellow in need knows that he is not losing, but his generosity and sharing
will be reciprocated. Thus, one is not to complain about a debt if he or she knows the debtor
for an act of generosity is never a loss. It may profit generations to come.

Resources

Internet:
Easylinks and updates for the following websites at donnaward.net

Employment Intensive Investment Programme. Strategy to invest in employment instead of heavy equipment.
National Geographic Congo Trek 360.
The Rainforest Foundation.
Baka Pygmies of Cameroon.
Strange Case of Ota Benga. Listen to a PBR broadcast about a pygmy who was taken to New York in 1904.
Creation Research, Ota Benga. Read how this case is evidence of racialism in Darwinism.

Books:
National Geographic Adventure magazine, March/April 2000. "Crazy in the Congo."
National Geographic magazine, July 1995. "Ndoki—Last Place on Earth."
Mankell, Henning. *Secrets in the Fire.* Based on the indomitable spirit of a real-life land mine victim (Ages 12+). Set in East
        Africa in Tanzania, but brings life to the chapter "War in the Hills" about Rwanda.

African Folktales:
Aardema, Verna. *Sebgugugu the Glutton : a Bantu tale from Rwanda* (Ages 5-12).
Aardema, Verna. *Tales For The Third Ear, From Equatorial Africa* (Ages 5-12).
Aardema, Verna. *Traveling To Tondo : A Tale Of The Nkundo Of Zaire* (Ages 5-12).
Mandela, Nelson (ed). *Nelson Mandela's Favorite African Folktales* (All ages).
Washington, Donna L. *A Pride of African Tales.* Six African stories with beautiful illustrations. (Ages 8-14)
Mitchison, Amanda. *Who Was David Livingstone* (Ages 8-12).

Films:
National Geographic Africa: Episode 3–Voices of the Forest. The Baka people of the tropical rainforest go on a hunt for
        game with a single bullet. They find loggers in their territory. Highly Recommended.
National Geographic Africa: Episode 6—Restless Waters. A fisherman on Lake Victoria, and a rice farmer in Tanzania
        both struggle to make a living.

Photograph previous page: Mount Cameroon as seen from Tiko, Southwest Province, Cameroon

📖 Read a book, or view a film or website about the gorillas and chimpanzees of the African Rainforest.

At one point, the lively missionary speaker brandished an executioner's knife that had, at one point, been too close to his own neck. He had fended off crocodiles and shot hippos to feed starving villagers. Complete with killer bees, tsetse flies, and dangerous wildlife, the jungle was a dark and perilous place. The stories of William Shepherd, black missionary to the Congo, further confirmed that the rainforest of equatorial Africa was a place of dangerous mystery at the turn of the 19th century.

Today, while much reduced by logging and farming, the rainforest still continues to confound the outsider. With unrest in the Democratic Republic of Congo (formerly Zaire) and poachers who stalk the forest, it is still dangerous. Probably the least troublesome are the forest dwellers, the gentle giant-hearted pygmies who hunt and gather in the forest.

The Congo River Basin is home to the endangered lowland gorilla, chimpanzees, a host of monkeys, and the unusual bongo, a hoofed animal with beautiful stripes. The climate is hot and humid, supporting abundant growth, and a host of birds and insects. Beyond the rainforest, the land rises to savanna plateaus in the north and south, and mountains in

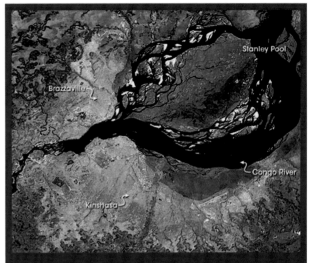

The capital city of the Congo is Brazzaville, on the north side of the Congo River. Directly opposite, Kinshasa is the capital city of the DR Congo. Livingstone Falls is the series of rapids which make the river impassable downstream from these cities as it flows toward the sea. Pool Malebo, formerly called Stanley Pool after explorer Henry M. Stanley, is a wide, lake-like portion of the Congo River.

the east. In the elevated regions the climate is cooler in the dry season and hot and humid in the rainy season. Visitors can pay a hefty fee to glimpse the endangered mountain gorilla in the forested mountains of Rwanda. Central Africa is still one of the most exotic and mysterious places on earth.

Look at your political map to see the narrow strip of land by which the Democratic Republic of Congo controls the lower Congo River as it empties into the Atlantic Ocean.

Internet Links: Go to **AWF Mountain Gorilla** to listen to noises gorillas make. Visit **Congo Pages** for pictures of the Congo. Easylink to these and other sites at **donnaward.net**

✏️ Use an atlas to write the names of the following countries (and capital cities) on your political map. Burundi, Cameroon, Central African Republic, Republic of Congo, Democratic Republic of Congo, Equatorial Guinea, Gabon, Rwanda, Sao Tomé and Principé.

Miniature Hunters of the Rainforest

 Look at books or websites about the people of the African rainforest.

The Pygmies of Central Africa are people who are typically less than 1.5 meters/5 feet in height. Traditionally they are nomadic hunters and gatherers in the rainforest. The various groups differ in language and tradition, but they are united in the fact that they are smaller than most people, and their traditional lifestyle is slowly disappearing.

Speak up for those who cannot speak up themselves; ensure justice for those being crushed. Yes, speak up for the poor and helpless, and see that they get justice.
Proverbs 31:8-9

Outsiders may find the jungle impenetrable, but these forest dwellers intimately know the footpaths, valleys, and rivers. They recognize the jungle noises when the deep quiet is broken by screeching birds or screaming monkeys. They respect that dangers may lurk around each turn, from leopards to deadly snakes. Skilful hunters and trackers, pygmies can accurately shoot down a plump bird or a monkey, or climb a tree to gather honey. They discern which forest plants are good to eat and which are poisonous. Termites and other insects are also a source of food. Pygmies will leave the rainforest to trade with neighboring villagers for plantains and other supplies, but then they generally retreat back to the sanctity of the rainforest.

The African Pygmies are known particularly for their exceptional vocal music which is often accompanied by stringed bows, harps, and wooden flutes. Water drumming, one of their most unique forms of music, is done while standing in a river. Players produce unique rhythms and sounds together by slapping the water. You should try this in a pool or bathtub (Close the bath curtain. It will be messy!).

The lifestyle of the forest dwellers is threatened by the shrinking of the forest. Logging is especially problematic as the companies open huge tracts of land with noisy machinery which greatly reduces the supply of game. Loggers bring tobacco and marijuana instead of food to trade, introduce diseases formerly unknown in the forest, and often poach, reducing the already declining animal population. Meat is becoming increasingly scarce.

Central African governments, while creating pre-served forest land for endangered wildlife, have given no land protection rights to the forest people. Instead, governments encourage permanent settlements to replace nomadic living. The pygmies hold an inferior place in society and, being thus disadvantaged, they prefer the peace of the forest as long as they can continue their lifestyle there.

Pygmy houses made with sticks and leaves in the northern area of the Republic of the Congo

Internet Links: Go to **Baka Pygmies** of Cameroon or **The Rainforest Foundation** to read more about these interesting people. Find out about their forests at **National Geographic Congo Trek**. Listen to The Strange Case of Otto Bengo and hear about a pygmy who was taken to New York in 1904. Discover how this event confirms racialism in Darwinism **Creation Research-Ota Benga**. Easylink to these sites at **donnaward.net**

View *National Geographic Africa*: Episode 3–Voices of the Forest. Complete a *Facts About People* notebook page about Pygmy group in Africa.

Intrepid Explorer and Missionary - David Livingstone

📖 Read *Exploring Africa* p. 32 or another book about David Livingstone or missionaries/explorers of Africa.

> I saw the lion behind the bush, and said, "Stop 'till I load again." When ramming down the bullets, I heard a shout. I saw the lion springing upon me. He caught my shoulder, and we both came to the ground. Growling horribly, he shook me as a terrier does a rat. The lion immediately left me, and, attacking Mebalwe, bit his thigh. Another man, whose life I had saved after he had been tossed by a buffalo, attempted to spear the lion. He (lion) left Mebalwe and caught this man by the shoulder, but at that moment the bullets he had received took effect, and he fell down dead.[1]

This story is just one of many in the grand adventures of Dr. David Livingstone in Africa. He traveled an amazing 46,670 km/29,000 miles in difficult, dangerous conditions for over thirty years.

Three goals grew in the mind of David Livingstone. Challenged as a young man by the great missionary, Dr. Robert Moffat, Livingstone could see the 'smoke of a thousand villages' where the gospel had never been preached. His heart burned with the passion to take God's love to the tribes of Africa. Then, as he traveled throughout Africa and saw the misery caused by the slave trade, he became fervent in seeking to crush this practice for "did not Jesus come to proclaim liberty to the captives?" Finally, he was convinced that if the land could be opened to honest business, there would be no need to continue to trade in human lives. He sought to abolish the slave trade.

An intrepid explorer, Livingstone was compelled to look for river sources and to travel where no white people had gone before, in the hopes of opening the land to missionaries and business. He recorded the geographic wonders of the land and unique customs of the people who lived in it.

David Livingstone always treated his black companions with the utmost respect and care. He sought to avoid war in every encounter. In one instance, while crossing the Zambezi River, he suspected the local chief had given the order to kill him and his troop. The threatening natives came to the river bank armed with spears. Livingstone waited until his party had crossed, staying behind until the last. Then he took out his watch and explained how it could tell the time. The natives came around close, listening and asking questions. Livingstone finished with "I wish you peace," and he crossed the river without a spear raised to harm him.

Early in his career, David Livingstone's wife and one child had died in Africa, and the rest of the children had returned to England. While his African guides were extremely loyal, Dr. Livingstone traveled all those years without English-speaking companions. He was ill much of the time, but doggedly persevered. When Livingstone had not been heard from in over three years an American, Henry Morton Stanley, was sent to search for him. Stanley found Livingstone in central Africa and, upon coming into the clearing to meet him, put out his hand and said those simple but famous words, "Dr. Livingstone, I presume?"

On his few homeland visits, Dr. Livingstone awed English audiences. He stood before them, his body haggard from tropical disease and his arm stiff from the wounds of the lion, and mesmerized the audience with stories full of zeal and danger. Announcing his impending return to Africa he said, "I return without misgiving and with gladness of heart. What supported me through all the years? It was this: Lo, I am with you always, even unto the end of the world! On those words I staked everything and they never failed!"

David Livingstone clung to that favorite Bible verse in all his difficulties, illness, and loneliness. After 30 years in Africa, his attendants, Chuma and Susi, found him kneeling by his bed where he had died in prayer. They faithfully took his body to the coast where it was sent to England. David Livingstone was buried with great honor at Westminster Abbey.

1 *A Popular Account of Dr. Livingstone's Expedition to the Zambesi and Its Tributaries And of the Discovery of Lakes Shirwa and Nyassa, 1858-1864* (David Livingstone's Journal).

✏️ Complete a *Facts About People* notebook page on David Livingstone.

Look at photos of Rwanda in books or online.

Rwanda is a small mountainous country in the middle of Africa. It has beautiful green landscape and pleasant tropical weather. In 1994, the Tutsi genocide marred this paradise and scarred the memory of its inhabitants forever. Crushing the lives of one million people in only three months, it became the war where the greatest number of lives was lost in the shortest time in the history of modern African conflict.

On April 6, 1994, a plane was shot from the sky, killing both the President of Rwanda and the President of neighboring Burundi. Like a stick of dynamite this event ignited carnage throughout Rwanda. How did it all start? For centuries there had been an ethnic conflict between the stocky Hutus, who were generally farmers, and the taller Tutsi people, who have traditionally been cattle herders. The Tutsis, though the minority, ruled the Hutus prior to, and through the colonial period, when first Germany and then Belgium controlled Rwanda.

In 1962, Rwanda gained independence and the Hutus grabbed the power, violently driving the Tutsis out of the country. For years the refugees lived in exile in countries around Rwanda. Refugees were denied the opportunity to return to their homes. For this reason the Rwandan Patriotic Front (RPF) was formed in 1990 and began to pressure the Rwandan government through armed conflict along the borders.

In 1993, the government and the RPF signed a cease-fire agreement which included the formation of a joint, power-sharing government. Politically moderate Hutus wanted this compromise so that there would be peace, but many extreme Hutus were vehemently opposed. These Hutu officials had been secretly training young men into armed groups called Interahamwe. They also launched a hate radio station aimed against Tutsis.

The death of the president unleashed the Interahamwe—young men, violent and full of hate. Hutu militants systematically hunted for Tutsi men, women, and children with the intent of exterminating them. All the moderate Hutus were also killed. The hate radio station urged Hutus to kill their Tutsi neighbors. Thousands were brutally murdered. The Tutsis, through the RPF, fought back, eventually taking power three months later, but not before over a million people had been massacred.

Afterwards, millions of Hutus feared the revenge of the surviving Tutsis and fled for their lives to refugee camps in neighboring countries. The Interahamwe were in the camps; there they harassed Hutu citizens and demanded loyalty or death.

The new Rwandan government, led by Paul Kagame, tried to eliminate racial divisions, stating that Rwandans were one united people, not Hutus nor Tutsis. The governing body contains a healthy mix of both Hutus and Tutsis. Now, years later, the people are rebuilding their country, but poverty, trauma, and loss of family members continues to grieve the survivors. The country is regarded as a safe place for tourists, and the government is working towards improving the lives of all its citizens.

In the neighboring Democratic Republic of Congo, many Rwandan dissidents live as refugees and continue to harass and kill Tutsis who live there. They are still a threat to the stability of Rwanda.

The Road to Ruhengeri - Rwanda

Internet Links: **Frontline 100 Days of Slaughter** gives a chronological outline of events in Rwanda in 1994. Find out the legal significance of using the term "genocide" instead of "war" in relation to U.N. responsibility. Listen to 1994 audio newscasting with slides at BBC (parental review recommended). Easylinks at **donnaward.net**

View *Africa, A Land of Hope*: Episode 6–Rwandan Diary.

Can You Give Me a Job?

📖 Enjoy a resource about Africa or play some internet map games to learn countries and capital cities.

Dawn was rising over the grassland as we drove from Jomo Kenyatta International Airport into the busy heart of Nairobi. We had traveled all night from England, so we were ready for bed just as Nairobi was up and moving (or not moving if you were stuck in a traffic jam). What did I notice first? People! Lots and lots of people walking along the road or on footpaths to the road. "Are there always so many people walking?" I asked the driver. "Or is it just the hour many are going to work?" "Always lots of people on the road," he replied. Many don't have jobs and are always walking, walking, looking for work."

In Africa there are many, many laborers, but not enough jobs. A few decades ago, in an effort to improve services such as roads or water systems, developing nations often borrowed money and purchased heavy equipment for construction. The result was high debt and equipment eventually in disrepair.

Why not use what they already have? People are the wealth of Africa. Would it not make sense to employ people instead of purchasing heavy machinery? The idea was tested and developed through the 1970s to 1990s. Instead of using back hoes and bulldozers, people were employed to load dump trucks and spread materials on roads. Instead of rock crushers to create gravel, men were given hammers and a pile of rock to break down. It was found that the overall cost of a project could be 10 - 30% lower, the foreign money needed was typically 50 - 60% less and the number of people with employment rose dramatically. This is described as labor-based technology, or, employment intensive programs.

The studies found that in order not to draw people from other jobs such as farming, the pay for workers in these projects had to be very minimal. Training became imperative for the engineers, politicians, and designers. It is usually an engineer's goal to develop tools and machinery which will decrease the number of people needed to do a job, while increasing speed and quality. You can see how an engineer would need new training on how to use more labor and less machinery in an efficient manner. Some universities in developing countries are now introducing labor-based technology courses into their engineering programs.

Many countries in Africa are successfully implementing employment intensive programs to complete road work and other improvement projects. This is creating much needed jobs and using their country's greatest resource - people!

A work crew spreads gravel in a road resurfacing project.

Jesus said:
The spirit of the Lord is upon me, for he has anointed me to bring Good News to the poor. He has sent me to proclaim that captives will be released, that the blind will see, that the oppressed will be set free.
Luke 4:18-19

Internet Links: **Employment Intensive Investment Programme.** Strategy to invest in employment instead of heavy equipment. Easylink to this site at **donnaward.net**

 View *National Geographic Africa*: Episode 6–Restless Waters.

Minding Money

📖 Look at some advertisements in any type of media: magazine, T.V., or newspapers. Discuss advertisers' methods.

When we discern that most people in the world live on a bare fraction of what we spend in a year, it becomes all the more imperative for us to be wise stewards with our wealth. If you have a home with a garage and a car you are among the world's wealthiest 5%.

> If someone has enough money to live well and sees a brother or sister in need but shows no compassion – how can God's love be in that person?
> I John 3:17

Spend carefully and don't be frivolous or excessive. Have a plan: 10/10/80 is reasonable. The first 10% is given to God. Become a contributor instead of a consumer. The next 10% is savings for the future. (Some financial advisors suggest young people should save 50% of their income for their education.) The final 80% is what we should live on. As a working adult, you may find you can live on less than 80% and share an increasingly higher portion with the needy. Many people spend 100% or 110% of their income for their living expenses, and then try to give and save. It doesn't work. Strive to live simply and within your means. If you wish to make a large purchase, be patient and save before you buy. Don't borrow money to get things quickly.

Never make a large purchase "on the spot." Anyone who pressures you to buy immediately knows that if the sale isn't sealed right away, you may not buy. If this is the case it may not be such a "good deal" after all. Develop a cooling off period and always tell the vendor, "I would like to

Ask Before You Buy....
Do I really need it? Can I afford it?
Could I borrow one from a friend or neighbor?
Do I have one already that could be repaired?
How long will it probably last? Can I maintain it?
What are ALL the costs over its lifetime?
How many hours or months will I have to work to pay for it? Is it worth it?
Is it recyclable?
Give yourself a 48-hour "cooling off" period to think about it before you buy (30 days for a major purchase).

think about this and research it a bit more. **I will call you** when I decide."

Did you know that during the early years of T.V. there was no children's programming? Children's programming started when people wanted to sell their products. The first T.V. cartoons were created specifically to sell sugared cereals.

Today's ads are a lot different from the ones 20 years ago. In the old ads, parents were portrayed as pillars of wisdom. Now, advertisers portray parents as "out of touch" and dumb, so that children are encouraged to ignore their parents' efforts to protect them from commercial pressure. Privately, advertisers plan how to minimize parental influence so that children can be "captured, owned, and branded" and thus succumb to advertising gimmicks. Advertising will affect you. Be prepared.

AdBusters is an activist cause aimed at reducing the influence and prevalence of advertising and consumerism. Here is one of their Joe Chemo ads spoofing the Joe Camel Tobacco campaign that was criticised for advertising tobacco to children. This is a true picture

of the results of tobacco use, but not the one the tobacco companies would want us to see. AdBusters has promoted a "Buy Nothing Day" every November which is gaining publicity around the world. Do you think this is an effective method to help people think about overspending? Why or why not?

Internet Links: **Adbusters Videos.** Watch the **humorous but significant "Buy Nothing Day Pig"** Video and be part of the growing movement to curb consumerism. Easylink to this site at **donnaward.net**

Discuss your family's lifestyle. What are the ways you can minimize the effect of advertising and minimize spending? Review your personal budget for money you earn or receive, or make a budget if you do not have one.

East Africa

Chagga Proverb
(Tanzania)

Usipopata taabu hujawa Intu (Swahili).

Endurance is paramount to attaining success or perfection.

The Chagga are a Bantu people whose homeland stretches across the slopes of Africa's highest mountain, Kilimanjaro, in northeastern Tanzania. They practice mixed farming and believe in a worldview that integrates life's hardships as unavoidable co-building blocks of a successful life. This Chagga saying expresses, in a nutshell, their philosophy and theology of life vis-a-vis suffering; it is often repeated to youngsters, as well as to old folks who find life's dealings too difficult to bear, in order to encourage them to persevere and to carry on. Success stories of persons who have made it in life through sheer struggle (or suffering) are much extolled among the Chagga people. By using this saying such persons are looked upon as heroes which others can imitate.

Resources

Internet:
Easylinks and updates for the following websites at donnaward.net

Samsays Safari Photographs. Great photos taken in Kenya on safari.
Peter Andzel Travel Photography. Photos of Madagascar.
Serengeti National Park Official Site. Play the animal sound game.
Imagico Views of the Earth. Computer generated pictures of the Great Rift Valley.
Greatest Places Madagascar for interesting information about this island.
Maasai Laleyio. Best site for information and music of the Maasai people.

Books:
Bateman, Robert. *Safari*. Beautiful paintings and interesting text about the animals on the savanna (All ages).
Dinesen, Isak. *Out of Africa*. Chapters about separate events. Read excerpts. Beautiful word pictures (Advanced listeners).
Dunph, Madeleine. *Here is the African Savanna*. Picture book (Ages 3-8).
Feelings, Muriel. *Jambo Means Hello, Swahili Alphabet Book*. Traditional African life through Swahili (Ages 5-12).
Joosse, Barbara M. *Papa, Do You Love Me?* Masai lifestyle illustrated in a Papa's unconditional love (Ages 5-10).
Kessler, Christina. *My Great-Grandmother's Gourd*. Desert traditions and new ways. A true story (Ages 5-12).
Kroll, Virginia. *Masai and I* (Ages 5-10).
Mankell, Henning. *Secrets in the Fire*. Based on the indomitable spirit of a real-life land mine victim (Ages 12+).
McCall Smith, Alexander. *Akimbo and the Crocodile Man* (Ages 5-12).
McCall Smith, Alexander. *Akimbo and the Lions* (Ages 5-12).
McCall Smith, Alexander. *Akimbo and the Elephants* (Ages 5-12).
Shah, Anup & Manoj. *The Circle of Life: Wildlife on the African Savannah*. Spectacular photos/informative text.
Whelan, Gloria. *Listening for Lions*. Heartwarming fiction of a missionary girl during colonial times (Ages 8-12).

African Folktales:
Aardema, Verna. *Bim wili & the Zimwi: a tale from Zanzibar* (Ages 5-12).
Aardema, Verna. *How The Ostrich Got A Long Neck: A Tale From The Akamba Of Kenya* (Ages 5-12).
Aardema, Verna. *Rabbit Makes A Monkey Of Lion: A Swahili Tale* (Ages 5-12).
Aardema, Verna. *The Lonely Lioness And The Ostrich Chicks: A Masai Tale* (Ages 5-12).
Aardema, Verna. *What's So Funny, Ketu?* (Ages 5-12).
Aardema, Verna. *Who's In Rabbit's House?: A Masai Tale* (Ages 5-12).
Mandela, Nelson (ed). *Nelson Mandela's Favorite African Folktales* (All ages).
Mollell, Tololwa M. *Big Boy*. African theme in contemporary setting (Ages 5-10).

Films:
Out of Africa, starring Meryl Streep/Robert Redford Note: the book is about the land and the African people. The
     movie is about Karen Blixen. The book is better, but scenery in the movie is great (Please preview).
National Geographic Africa: Episode 1—Savanna Homecoming; Episode 4—Mountains of Faith;
     Episode 7—Leopards of Zanzibar
Endurance. Inspiring true story of Ethiopian long-distance runner Haile Gebrsellasie's life outlines the numerous trials
     and tribulations he had to overcome to win Olympic gold at Atlanta in 1996.

Geography of East Africa

 View *Africa, A Land of Hope*: Epsiode 7–A Visit to Kenya

The ugly forms trot in the semi-light, pausing here and there to inspect the air. Wary, the hyenas keep a brisk pace past the two lions, which stretch while the African dawn softens the chill. Their foraging done, the hyenas hurry to their den while the lions begin the day by gazing intently across the plain. Gazelles graze, moving on delicate feet. Is there a weak one among them? A drama will play out today across the savanna, as it does every day; the hunted and the hunters in a life and death dance. The lion is king in the East African grasslands.

The Great Rift Valley of East Africa provides spectacular vistas, including some of the deepest lakes in the world and Mount Kilimanjaro, the tallest free-standing mountain. South of the Ethiopian highlands, the valley splits into the East Rift and the West Rift, with Lake Victoria between them.

The climate in the elevated area is very comfortable and remains temperate most of the year, unlike the coastal regions, which can be hot and humid. East Africa is exceptionally suitable for farming and thus became a target for colonization.

The large island of Madagascar is home to some unique animals which originate only on Madagascar.

Elephants in Amboseli National Park at the base of Kilimanjaro

The most notable is the Lemur, a primate which is found in fifty colorful variations. Lemurs are endangered and some species are extinct because so much of their habitat is being destroyed. Madagascar is a mix of coastal rainforest and high plateau.

Ethiopian Highlands

Scenic lookout of the Great Rift Valley in Kenya

Sleeping Sickness is a hazard faced by the people and animals who live on the grassland of Africa. It is caused by a parasite carried by the Tsetse fly. Without treatment, this disease usually causes death. Find out how scientists are eliminating this threat. See "Sterile Atomic Fly" at Wikipedia Online Encyclopedia.

Internet Links: **Imagico Views of the Earth.** 3-D Computer generated pictures of the Great Rift Valley. See **Greatest Places Madagascar** for interesting photos and information about this island. Easylink at **donnaward.net**

 Use an atlas to find and write the names of the following countries (and their capital cities) on your political map of Africa:
Comoros, Djibouti, Eritrea, Ethiopia, Kenya, Madagascar, Mauritius, Seychelles, Somalia, Sudan, Tanzania, Uganda.

The Maasai, Herders of the Savanna

📖 Read a book about the Maasai people, or visit a website to see pictures and listen to music of the Maasai.

Bumping along the dirt track, we raced past elephants and giraffes wondering why Pilot, our driver, did not stop to show us these giants. "No problem," he called; "We'll come back. Trust me!" Twenty minutes into the setting sun of the savanna, we understood. There was a cheetah feasting in front of our eyes. "The kill is just an hour old," we were told. We learned to trust the knowledge of the drivers.
The next morning, a Maasai guide joined our driver. "Lions!" He pointed to sea of grass. We could only marvel as ten minutes later we caught up to a couple of lionesses and their cubs. How could this guide spot them from a great distance in all their camouflage?

Dance of young Maasai warriors

Herding cattle on the plains from the time they are young boys, the Maasai have intimate knowledge of the wildlife of the savanna. Traditionally, Maasai warriors would single-handedly hunt a lion prior to marriage. There are fewer lions today, but many of the Maasai have had to protect their cattle from lions at some time in their youth.

The Maasai people of Kenya and Tanzania, with their colorful clothing and unique, pastoral lifestyle, are one of the most widely known indigenous cultures of Africa. They have resisted schooling or change, and cling to their traditional ways. The sale of handicrafts has become a popular way of earning income.

Maasai men and women enjoy many traditional dances, the best known being the warrior "jumping dance" where young men leap straight into the air from a standing position to show their strength and agility.

Maasai life ultimately revolves around cattle, which are grazed over large areas of land in the Great Rift Valley. Four protected game

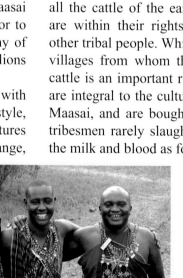
Nteka (left), the guide who spotted lions from a distance. Pilot (center) and Edward (right), our safari drivers.

reserves have reduced Maasai grazing land. Frequent drought creates hardship. The Maasai believe that all the cattle of the earth belong to them, and they are within their rights to reclaim cattle from any other tribal people. While this has led to friction with villages from whom they steal cattle, repossessing cattle is an important rite for young warriors. Cattle are integral to the culture. They are currency for the Maasai, and are bought and sold as necessary. The tribesmen rarely slaughter their cattle; but they use the milk and blood as food.

Maasai huts are built from branches woven together with grass and sealed with dried cow dung. The homes are built around an inner kraal made of thorny branches where the cattle are protected for the night. Another hedge of branches surrounds the village to protect the people and livestock from marauding hyenas, leopards, and lions.

"Meishoo iyiook enkai inkishu o-nkera"—a Maasai prayer, "May Creator give us cattle and children.

Internet: **Maasai Laleyio.** Best site for information and music of the Maasai. Also visit the **Maasai Association** site and look for the reason the Maasai prefer the spelling of their name with two 'a's instead of one as in Masai. Advanced listeners hear the African correspondent describe **Africa's Lagging Development-"Solutions to Africa's Food Woes Remain Elusive"** at National Public Radio. Easylinks at **donnaward.net**

 Complete a *Facts About People* notebook page of the Maasai people of Kenya and Tanzania.

Colonialism, Control and Corruption

📖 Look at one of the following: *Exploring Africa* p. 42, *Listening to Lions, Out of Africa* or *Matatu Magic* (see below)

In 1931, coffee farmer, Karen Blixen, sold her farm near Nairobi. The Kikuyu who had worked that farm were forced to relocate, but where would they go? She writes, "They had lived in the illusion that the land was theirs....The Natives cannot, according to the law, themselves buy any land.... I told them that they must go into the Kikuyu Reserve and find land there. They gravely asked me if they should find enough unoccupied land in the Reserve to bring all their cattle with them. And would they be sure all to find land in the same place, so that the people from the farm should remain together, for they did not want to be separated? It is more than their land that you take away from the people, whose Native land you take. It is their past as well, their roots and their identity. Now, my squatters were clinging to one another....If they were to go away from their land, they must have people around them who had known it, and so could testify to their identity. As it was, they were feeling the shame of extinction falling on them."[1]

In the nineteenth century the European thirst to explore unknown places caused adventurers to set out on relentless quests into the interior of Africa. Missionaries established outposts and traders searched for wealth in the resources of the land.

The Americas were now settled, and European nations saw Africa as the new continent to control. They jostled each other in what has been called "The Scramble for Africa," with the result that in 20 short years the continent was divided up and ruled by colonial powers. Borders were arbitrary and resistance by Africans was quickly crushed. Indigenous Africans were pushed off their lands, restricted, and given few civil rights. Eventually, an African resistance arose to speak out against discrimination and demand freedom from colonial rule. Independence in Africa began with Libya in 1951. Many countries followed in the '50s and '60s, often as a result of violent struggle.

During colonial rule, the traditional tribal economy had been shattered, and dependency on European business had been established. Dependency is still a problem in Africa. Much of the economy had been built for European interests. Railways always led to the coast as Europeans exported goods to Europe.

Today, trade between African nations is hindered by poor transportation routes within Africa itself.

After independence, lack of good education held back development. Many new country leaders had been in powerful military positions, but were not educated about how to govern a country. National borders, which had been drawn up by European rulers, disregarded traditional ethnic divisions, and the resulting tribal conflict continues to produce violence and uncertainty in many countries today.

Following independence, most African countries have been troubled by war, corruption, and poor government. Corruption has been one of the most harmful components hindering improvement. Organizations, such as Transparency International, have done much to expose and reduce it. Journalists are beginning to speak out against corruption where they can. Citizens are educated about the detriment of giving bribes for services.

In the annual Corruption Perceptions Index, Transparency International has consistently found that most African countries rank very low on the corruption scale. The organizations which frequently require bribes for services are often the police, city officials, educators, and hospitals. By exposing this problem, greater accountability can be realized.

In Kenya, where few people own cars, privately owned minivans, called matatus, act as public transportation. If you rode a matatu before 2004, you would never be sure of the cost of the fare; you might end up with two people on your lap, or the driver may be abusive. The matatu would also have to stop frequently for the driver to pay illicit "road tax" along the way. Notorious for overcharging, overloading, speeding, disobeying traffic laws, using unsafe vehicles, and verbally abusing passengers, matatu drivers were responsible for many deaths and injuries on the road each year.

In 2004, the Kenyan government clamped down on unsafe public transportation. Drivers and conductors were required to wear uniforms and be permanent employees. Matatus had to install speed governors to limit speeds to 80 kph/50 mph or less. All passengers have to wear a seatbelt and passengers may not stand. Fares could not change and routes had to be posted in the vehicle window. This is one way the government has helped reduce corruption and improve safety. The riders are very thankful.

1 Dinesen, Isak. *Out of Africa,* "Farewell to the Farm." 1960, p. 387.

Internet Links: Listen to a radio drama from **BBC, Matatu Magic**. While matatus have been known to cause deaths and injuries on the roads, no one dies in this five part series. For answers to many questions about Karen Blixen, author of *Out of Africa,* see **Karen Blixen-Isak Dinesen Information Site. Transparency International Corruption Index** can be found along with other sites on the Easylinks at **donnaward.net**

Animals of the Savanna

📖 Enjoy the many books and films from your local library on African wildlife.

On an African game reserve you can see some of the largest animals on earth. You will see herbivores like the grazing zebras and nibbling gazelles, and the carnivores that hunt them, like the lion or cheetah. The herbivores need to eat continually all day to gain enough food for their energy needs. Think about this! An elephant has to eat about 100–200kg/220–440lb of food a day! Measure your own weight to get some idea of how much this is. Elephants need a lot of food! Most herbivores are social and live in groups.

Forget about grass! The carnivore prefers meat. These predators hunt in the cool of the day, looking for the weak or young. Lions are social, hunting and living together in a pride. A cheetah, the fastest mammal on earth, can be both solitary and social. Leopards, the smallest of the big cats, are solitary and nocturnal. They hunt at night, and sleep in the day in trees, bushes, or behind rocks.

The scavengers–the vultures and hyenas–clean up the leftovers after the carnivores are done.

Note: The Game Park, Masai Mara, uses the British spelling of Masai with one 'a'. The Maasai people prefer their name to be spelled with the double 'a' and the accent to fall on the first syllable in keeping with their language.

Internet Links: **Serengeti National Park Official Site.** Play the animal sounds game. Easylink at **donnaward.net**

The Big Five
The 'Big Five' animals of Africa are the elephant, rhinoceros, leopard, lion, and buffalo. They are named not for their size, but because they are dangerous animals which will attack if they feel threatened. Tourists "on safari" are hoping to see the "Big Five" and the savanna has become the area most visited by tourists.

Herbivores
- giraffe
- impala
- gazelle
- buffalo
- elephant
- wildebeest
- zebra
- rhinoceros
- hippopotamus

Predators
- lions
- cheetah
- leopard
- wild dogs

Scavengers
- vultures
- hyenas

Serengeti Proverb
Every morning in Africa, a gazelle wakes up. It knows it must run faster than the fastest lion or it will be killed. Every morning a lion wakes up. It knows that it must outrun the slowest gazelle or it will starve to death. It doesn't matter whether you are a lion or a gazelle, when the sun comes up, you'd better be running.

The Serengeti is a large national game reserve in Tanzania, connecting with the Masai Mara game reserve in Kenya. This is the site of the annual wildebeest migration.

You can see that the wildebeest are keeping a close eye on this lion. Wildebeest is a favorite food for lions.

 Pick your favourite African animals of the savanna and spend a few days reading and completing *Animal Facts* pages.

Hunger & Hope in an Urban Slum

Measure the smallest bedroom in your home. If it is bigger than 2.4 m/8 ft. by 1.8 m/6 ft., it is bigger than most homes in Mathare Valley. Each home is usually shared by six to eight people. Try to get comfortable with four to six people in one double bed.

I closed the door but it fell inward. "Here," said the pastor as he caught it. "This is how you do it." He gently lifted the door into place. No hinges; no way to lock it. Will this grandmother and her grandchildren be safe at night, in a place where criminals rule and the desperate roam? Six people shared this space that had four seats and one double bed.

Children look at used clothing for sale on a street in the Valley.

Pastor Daniel (left), teachers, students and guests gather in the school courtyard to pose with the valued music trophy.

Near the centre of Nairobi, Mathare Valley is home to half a million people. It is the worst slum in Africa. The Nairobi River flows through the middle, bringing its collection of garbage and sewage. The slum rises on steep banks one hundred and fifty meters on each side, stretching down the stream for two kilometers.

Imagine putting 500,000 people, the whole population of a city like New Orleans, into a mall parking lot. Remove the pavement. Add a smelly stream, mud and tin shacks, a few PAY toilets, and taps to be shared by everyone, but no electricity! This is Mathare Valley!

The eyes of idle men, criminals, and drug addicts were on us as we descended the dirt path, avoiding the gutters full of sewage. Women sat in the dirt with infants at their skirts, some selling vegetables spread on a cloth. The dirty-faced children flocked to us with smiles, chiming "How are you? How are you?" We slapped their hands in greeting but kept moving. *Mzungus* (white people) only visit this place with escorts–young men from the Mathare Community Outreach Church.

Through a maze between tin roofs, we reached the school where a concrete block room rose uncharacteristically like an oasis amidst the shanties. In a rough kitchen, ladies made breakfast and lunch to feed 1400 children, who might otherwise receive no nourishment for the day.

Over nine hundred youngsters, many sponsored through Compassion, sit in the crowded classrooms, anxious for an education. Christian teachers, underpaid but dedicated, instruct in academics and the Bible. In 2006, for the first time, the choirs from this project won various awards, advancing all the way to the national level. The large trophy they prize is a symbol of great accomplishment for children, many of whom are orphans, and are on the bottom of the heap in their society.

Mathare Valley is a place despised by most Kenyans, but not by Pastor and Mrs. Daniel Ogutu who left professional careers to follow God's call to these forgotten people. Families are changed

Pastor Daniel & Mrs. Magdaline Ogutu

through the gospel of Jesus. Some school children are able to leave the valley to go to high school. Destitute people are reaching out to help their own neighbours.

At Mathare Community Outreach Program the light of Jesus shines in a very dark place and there is hope where there was once only despair.

View *Africa, A Land of Hope*: Episode 8–Hunger in the Slums

Harriet Mutumba - Sponsorship to Sponsor

Born in a poor suburb of Kampala, Uganda, Harriet Mutumba faced huge obstacles in her life. As a child growing up in a family of seven children, Harriet struggled for anything of her own. Her father, owner of a vegetable stall, made a meagre income while her mother stayed home to take care of the children.

The consequences of poverty were amplified when young Harriet went to school. Instead of being praised for her potential, Harriet was singled out for her poverty.

"My most painful memory is when one of my classmates said my family must be really poor since my dad had only one pair of trousers," the 25-year-old recalls. "I decided then to never speak up in class and I began to dread going to school." Her shame at being poor drowned out her self-esteem.

Though life was difficult for young Harriet, there was one place that served as her oasis from crushing poverty –her Compassion project.

"When I got into the program of Compassion, I got photos from my sponsor and I was very excited," Harriet says. "I thought at least it's someone …. even if it's not someone that stays near me or someone that is in my class or in my school or in my community or in my country; there's someone out there who loves me."

Harriet's earthly trials continued after she became a Christian. When she was 15, her father walked out on his wife and seven children. "I looked at him as a traitor," Harriet said. "I felt he had betrayed us. How could he?" After Harriet's father left, the family was forced to move into a one-room shack fashioned out of rotten wood and prone to leaks. "One day I made a joke and told my brother if I got a visitor when rain was falling, I would just tell the visitor to remain outside because even if they entered the house, they would still get wet. I felt so bad about staying in such a house."

Because her Compassion project paid for her school fees, Harriet began to shun her shame by going to school

and started to blossom academically. Harriet received another devastating blow when she didn't score high enough on her state exams to get a government scholarship to a university. "I was very sure that my parents could not afford to sponsor me at the university," said Harriet.

Through it all Harriet knew two things would never fail her—God's never-ending love and the support from Compassion and her sponsors. Soon after graduating from high school, Harriet was accepted into Compassion's Leadership Development Program (LDP).

The LDP program allowed her to obtain a university education as well as Christian leadership training which Harriet felt, gave her an advantage over her peers.

"Other students who are in university, but who are not in the Leadership Development Program, miss important skills," Harriet said. "Through LDP, we are trained to be an influential Christian leader—a servant leader—someone who will emulate Jesus as when He washed the feet of His disciples. I received discipleship skills. Not any student in university can get such skills."

Excelling at the Uganda Christian University in Kampala, Harriet went on to post-graduate studies in law and graduated with a law degree. Today, Harriet investigates complaints of family abuse, including domestic violence and child abuse, in her role as a lawyer with the Uganda Human Rights Commission. She interviews victims and counsels them to help change the culture of violence permeating the poor and vulnerable in her country.

Never one to forget what God has given her, Harriet now sponsors her own Compassion child—Bryan from Ecuador. "The Bible tells me, to whom much is given much is expected," Harriet says. "The Lord gave me a lot when I was still in the program of Compassion and He expects a lot from me. I am planning to use all the skills I gained to impact other peoples' lives."

Internet Links: For more stories go to **Compassion International—Leadership Development Program.** Easylink at **donnaward.net**

 View *Africa, A Land of Hope*: Episode 9–A New Generation of Leaders.

Southern Africa

Tswana Proverb
(Botswana)

Poo, ga di nne pedi mo sakeng.

Two bulls can't stay in the same kraal.

In an agricultural society like we have in most of the rural parts of Botswana,
animals are the measure of wealth. Historically, people have not trusted banks and choose instead to keep their
wealth in the form of cattle, sheep, goats and donkeys. Cattle are at the top of the list. There is an intimate
relationship between a person and his or her cattle. It is common knowledge that you cannot put
two bulls into one kraal. They will fight each other unto death. This proverb is used to
point out that you can't have it both ways. A decision has to be made.
While there may be two options, you must choose between them.

Resources

Internet:
Easylinks and updates for the following websites at donnaward.net

Greatest Places Namib
Greatest Places Okavango Delta
South Africa Info Photo galleries. Various galleries including Nelson Mandela, coastlines, wildlife.
Geographia. Search topics: Namibia, Botswana, Zimbabwe.
Aids in Africa Online Resource. Animated maps and diagrams make statistics behind HIV/AIDS in Africa more engaging.
Kids Health HIV and AIDS. Good explanations for kids on the immune system and HIV/AIDS.
National Geographic Bushmen. Bushmen of the Kalahari.
NPR Series: Africa's Lagging Development. Advanced Listeners: "Under Dictator, Zimbabwe Slides into Chaos"
      Very interesting radio series. Insight into how bad government hinders development.

Books:
Kessler, Christina. *My Great-Grandmother's Gourd*. Desert traditions and new ways. A true story (Ages 5-12).
Shoveller, Herb. *Ryan and Jimmy and the Well in Africa That Brought Them Together.* A true story for 2006 (All ages).
Sisulu, Elinor. *The Day Gogo Went to Vote*. Moving tale of an historic event in South Africa (Ages 5-12).
Stanley, Diane. *Shaka, King of the Zulus* (Ages 5-12).
Holland, Gini. *Nelson Mandela* (Ages 8-12).
Deneberg, Barry. *Nelson Mandela; No Easy Walk to Freedom* (Ages 10+).
Hadland, Adrian. *Who Was Nelson Mandela?* (Ages 8-12).

Novels:
McCall Smith, Alexander. *Akimbo and the Crocodile Man* (Ages 5-12).
McCall Smith, Alexander. *Akimbo and the Lions* (Ages 5-12).
McCall Smith, Alexander. *Akimbo and the Elephants* (Ages 5-12).
Naidoo, Beverley. *Journey to Jo'Burg*. Life of apartheid in South Africa (Ages 8-12).
Naidoo, Beverley. *Chain of Fire*. Children resist the government forcing them to move to a "homeland" (Ages 8-12).
Naidoo, Beverley. *No Turning Back*. A moving glimpse into the life of Jo-burg's *malunde*, street children (Ages 8-12).
Naidoo, Beverley. *Out of Bounds, Seven Stories of Conflict and Hope*. Stories from the decades of apartheid (Ages 8-12).
Paton, Alan. *Cry, The Beloved Country*. A Zulu Christian Pastor's journey to Jo'burg in search of his son.
      Classic "must read" for older students (Also on film) (Ages 12 +).
Malan, Rian. *My Traitor's Heart*. An Afrikaner returns to South Africa just before the collapse of Apartheid. Drawing
      on the 300-year history of his family and current events, the author explains the enigma of apartheid (Adult).
McCall Smith, Alexander. *The #1 Ladies Detective Agency* A delightful way to learn culture (Age 12 +).
Stratton, Alan. *Chanda's Secret*. Chanda's mother is not herself, her younger sister is acting out, and her best friend
      needs help. A powerful story set amid the African HIV/AIDS pandemic (Age 14+).

Folktales:
Aardema, Verna. *Behind The Back Of The Mountain; Black Folktales From Southern Africa* (Ages 5-12).
Aardema, Verna. *Jackal's Flying Lesson : A Khoikhoi Tale* (Ages 5-12).
Aardema, Verna. *This For That : A Tonga Tale* (Ages 5-12).
Mandela, Nelson. *Nelson Mandela's Favorite African Folktales* (All ages).

Film:
The Interpreter (2005) - Political drama parallels Zimbabwe & Robert Mugabe (Adult) (see Wikipedia "The Interpreter").
National Geographic Africa. Episode 8–Southern Treasures.
National Geographic Videos. *The Kalahari Desert People.* 1975.
National Geographic Videos. *Bushmen of the Kalahari.* 1973.

Photograph previous page: False Bay on the way to Cape Point and Cape of Good Hope, South Africa.

Geography of Southern Africa

Read a selection from an Alexander McCall Smith book, or look at photos of the landscape of Southern Africa.

The most striking geographic feature of southern Africa is its elevation. It is shaped like an inverted saucer with a high center. The coastal lowlands rise abruptly to form a series of mountain ranges called the Great Escarpment with the highest elevations in the east, along the Indian Ocean. The inner part of the bowl is the central plateau. The higher southern area is called the Highveld. Veld is a term from the Afrikaans language meaning 'field.'

North of the Highveld is the Kalahari Basin which is still over 1000 meters above sea level and very sandy and dry. The Kalahari Basin contains the Kalahari Desert.

The vegetation of southern Africa ranges from forest and grassland to hot, dry desert. Rich mineral deposits of gold, diamonds, copper, and coal are found in southern Africa.

The Namib Desert with its extraordinary red sand

and huge dunes make it one of the most unusual places on earth. It runs in a narrow strip up the Atlantic coast. The winds blow from the land out to sea so that little or no rain falls. When the warm desert air meets the cold ocean current from the seas of Antarctica, constant fog is produced along the coast. Throughout sailing history, ships were wrecked on these shores, stranding sailors who had little hope of survival. Is it any wonder the north part of the coast of Namibia is called "The Skeleton Coast?"

The Kalahari Desert is a huge sandy wasteland with shrubs, acacia, and open grasslands. It is home to the San people, or bushmen, a semi-nomadic group who are expert hunters and gatherers. While the Kalahari has no permanent ground water, it is not a true desert as it receives enough rainfall to support vegetation.

Everything about the Kalahari is harsh. It can be extremely hot in the daytime and then drop to subzero night time temperatures. The land may be parched, but when the rains come, it is in torrential thunderstorms.

Animals struggle to survive not only the environment, but the advancement of man. There are a number of natural reserves to protect wildlife such as elephants, giraffes, lions, and cheetahs.

The Kalahari reveals its treasure in one of the biggest diamond mines in the world, the Orapa diamond mine in Botswana, co-owned by DeBeers Diamonds and the Botswana government.

Lesotho, the tiny mountain country, has two unique features. First, it is an enclave of South Africa, meaning it is completely surrounded by another, independent country.

Secondly, Lesotho is the highest country in the world, entirely above 1,000 meters/3,300 ft in elevation, with over eighty percent of the land 1800 meters/6600 ft above sea level. Snow is common on the mountains between May and September, with snow year-round on the higher peaks.

Internet Links: Interesting facts for kids at **Greatest Places Namib**, and **Greatest Places Okavango**. Check photographer's sites through Easylinks at **donnaward.net**

Use an atlas to write the names of the following countries (and their capital cities) on your *Political Map of Africa*:
Angola, Botswana, Lesotho, Malawi, Mozambique, Namibia, South Africa, Swaziland, Zambia, Zimbabwe.

Zulus and Xhosa, Then and Now

Read *Shaka, King of the Zulus* or another book or website about indigenous people of Southern Africa.

Southern Africa is home to many different cultures and dialects. Under Shaka Zulu, the Zulu kingdom became one of the most prominent nations in South Africa. Between 1816 and 1828, King Shaka transformed the small Zulu clans into a large military force. After his death, the Zulus continued to be one of the foremost forces which opposed white settlement. Today, Zulus are the most numerous ethnic group in South Africa. Ladysmith Black Mambazo is a Zulu music group renowned for bringing South African harmony to the world.

The Xhosa tribe is another major people group, most notably the heritage of Nelson Mandela, the great activist and first black president of South Africa. In South Africa, the Xhosa-speaking people form the second largest language group after Zulu. The Xhosa language contains an interesting variety of click sounds. The Xhosa people settled in areas where rich soil and plentiful rainfall made the land suitable for farming and grazing. As with many African herding cultures, wealth often still is counted in cattle.

In Botswana and Namibia, the Bushmen or San culture, also with a clicking language, is considered one of the oldest cultures in Africa. For thousands of years, the Bushmen of the Kalahari have lived as hunters and gatherers in the desert. The men make poison from grubs and acacia leaves and carefully dab it across arrow shafts. They are expert trackers, and can hunt and kill a large animal with small poisoned arrows. The women gather food. Roasted beetle and acacia leaves are a favorite delicacy when ground into a paste. It has been reported to taste similar to peanut butter. The Bushmen in Botswana are being forced off the free roaming lands into villages where they are taught farming and given cattle and goats. There is speculation that the government wants the land for tourism and diamond mining.

Dutch, British, and Indian settlers, who colonized southern Africa, make up a significant part of the population. The Dutch dialect of settlers in South Africa became known as Afrikaans, and descendents of the Dutch settlers are known as Afrikaners.

Ladysmith Black Mambazo

Black workers from southern c o u n t r i e s would travel by rail to work in the mines, far from their families and homes. They were poorly housed and poorly paid. After a six-day work week they would entertain themselves by singing and dancing into the wee hours of Sunday morning. Fearing the camp security guards, they called themselves "tip toe guys," referring to their soundless dance steps. When miners returned to the homelands, the music tradition and harmonies came with them.

The music of Ladysmith Black Mambazo was born in the mines of South Africa. The group has performed traditional and gospel music worldwide, including Disney's "The Lion King Part II" soundtrack.

Internet Links: Check **National Geographic Bushmen** for information about the dwellers of the Kalahari. Easylink at **donnaward.net**

 Complete a *Country Facts* notebook page about a Southern African country.

Finding Freedom with Nelson Mandela

📖 Read "The Typewriter" (1976) from *Out of Bounds,* or part of a book about Nelson Mandela.

In 1652, the Dutch set up a trading post called Cape Colony, where Dutch ships rounding the tip of Africa could stop to load up with food supplies. Dutch settlers, called Boers, began to arrive to establish farms. The Boers had many clashes with the African natives.

When British settlers began to arrive around 1820, the Boers balked at the strange language and to their shock, the British outlawed slavery. In response, thousands of Boers began to move inland on The Great Trek which continued from 1835 to 1843. Along the way, there were many bloody battles with the African Xhosa, Sotho, and Zulus. African spears were no match for the guns of the Boers, and in one bloody battle 3,000 Zulus were killed near a river which is called Blood River to this day.

The trekkers established the South African Republic, which is currently the area known as the Transvaal. They called themselves Afrikaners, claiming to be "the white tribe of Africa."

The British were completely uninterested in the Afrikaner states until Cecil Rhodes aggressively funded diamond mining in Transvaal. As the significance of the area grew, clashes with the Boers culminated in the Boer War. With a British victory in 1902, South Africa became part of the British Commonwealth.

The Boers and British remained bitter enemies. There were other problems after the war. Loyal blacks who had fought with the British in the Boer War were not given land and voting rights as they had expected. In 1912, a group who became known as the African National Congress (ANC), was organized to work for black civil rights. The white government began restricting the purchase of land by blacks, and blocked their ability to travel freely. This was the beginning of very bad times for blacks in South Africa. It grew extreme and intolerable when the Boer-led government came into power in 1948.

Nelson Mandela

This government enacted the law of apartheid, an Afrikaans term meaning "separateness." All people were classified by ethnic race; blacks had to carry passbooks, school was declared unnecessary for black children, and people were forced into slums called *townships*. The severe oppression led to many years of violence.

Nelson Mandela became a prominent leader in the struggle. He did not believe in extreme violence and promoted change by peaceful resistance. He was jailed for 30 years, emerging from prison in 1990 as one of the world's greatest heroes. In 1994 he was elected as the first black South African president. Today, he continues to expend great energy defending the disadvantaged.

Soweto (short for SOuth WEst TOwnship) is a large urban area of Johannesburg. The area is famous for riots between students and police in June, 1976. Mandela lived here for many years.

Internet Links: See **World Trek–Soweto**. For study of Mandela see **Frontline The Long Walk of Nelson Mandela**. Listen to a Soweto gospel choir. Easylink through **donnaward.net**

 Complete a *Facts About People* notebook page on Nelson Mandela.

Cecil Rhodes and the Mines

Look at a resource about Southern Africa.

Cecil Rhodes, a British teen visiting his brother in South Africa, decided to use the money his aunt had lent him to invest in diamond mining. What a success! He bought up smaller claims and purchased the mineral-rich farm of the de Beer brothers. Eventually Cecil Rhodes and his partner formed the De Beers Mining Company. Since that time it has had a monopoly on the diamond trade. Lack of competition allows the company to set prices at high rates. Only a few years after diamonds were found, South Africa boomed with the discovery of gold deposits.

Wishing to extend the British Empire into Africa, Cecil Rhodes moved into present day Zimbabwe and Zambia, and crushed all native resistance. British farmers then settled and established farms.

Many Africans left homes and families for years to work underground in the mines for poor pay.

The country to the north became Northern Rhodesia, after Cecil Rhodes, but was later renamed Zambia after achieving independence in 1964. The land south of the Zambezi River was named Rhodesia. Rhodesia was ruled by a white separatist government until the democratic elections in 1980, when Robert Mugabe was voted in as the head of state. The country was renamed Zimbabwe.

At this time, a small population of white farmers owned the largest percentage of land. The government ordered the land seized and redistributed. This resulted in a significant decrease in production. Robert Mugabe and his government have attracted international criticism for lack of good governance. Residents of Zimbabwe have struggled under both European and African rule.

Diamonds are Forever! Why are diamonds the gemstone most symbolic of eternity and love? In the 1930s, diamond sales were falling. The De Beers Group embarked on an aggressive marketing campaign with the slogan "diamonds are forever." They linked diamonds to movie stars, the British Royal Family, and to the concept of eternal love.

This campaign successfully limited the sale of previously owned diamond jewelry. (Ask your Mom if she would sell her diamond ring or buy a used diamond.) The advertisements also convinced buyers around the world that diamonds were the only appropriate wedding gemstone.[1]

Brilliant Cut diamonds

Witwatersrand

This is the name of a low mountain range in South Africa where Johannesburg has grown into a sprawling metropolis. In Afrikaans, Witwatersrand means the "ridge of white waters." Water that runs off to the north drains into the Indian Ocean and water running off to the south, drains into the Atlantic Ocean.

Witwatersrand is famous for being the location where almost 50% of the world's gold is mined. It is 100 km/60 miles long and in some places, up to 3.6 km/12,000 feet deep. It is no wonder the South African currency (money) is named the 'rand.'

Internet Links: Visit **PBS Nature Diamonds** for an interesting short video about diamond qualities. For deeper study, see the American Museum of Natural History site on **The Nature of Diamonds**. Find more links at Easylinks at **donnaward.net**

---

1 http://www.edwardjayepstein.com/diamond.htm. Accessed 20/11/06.

 View *National Geographic Africa*: Episode 8—Southern Treasure. Complete a *Facts About People* page for Cecil Rhodes.

Killer Disease

Check some internet resources to better understand the AIDS epidemic in Africa.

Achoo! You sneeze. Maybe it was dust and germs that your sneeze sent flying out of your body. If germs do get inside, then your immune system works to fight these invaders and keep your body healthy.

The Human Immunodeficiency Virus (HIV) is a virus that attacks a person's immune system. A person with HIV may feel just fine for a long time, but meanwhile the virus is slowly destroying the cells that fight bacteria in the body. When the immune system is finally completely weakened by HIV, the person will be diagnosed with Acquired Immunodeficiency Syndrome (AIDS) and their body is no longer able to fight disease. Once the disease advances to AIDS it is fatal. There is no cure.

HIV is passed from one person to another through sexual contact and through blood-to-blood contact, such as when someone uses unsterilized needles for tattoos, piercing, or illegal drugs. In addition, infected pregnant women can pass HIV to their babies during pregnancy or delivery, as well as through breast feeding.

AIDS is having a devastating effect in Africa. Southern Africa is one of the areas hardest hit. People have reported attending an average of two funerals per week.

- 70% of all AIDS affected adults live in Sub-Saharan Africa
- 12 million children have been orphaned by AIDS
- 2.3 million children have AIDS worldwide, 2.1 million of them in Africa

When parents die of AIDS, children are left grieving, with the struggle to survive, and no one to look after them. Traditionally, orphaned children in Africa are cared for by the extended family, but with aunts and uncles also affected, there are too few adults to care for all the orphans. Many single grandmothers are left with the burden of raising their grandchildren and they wonder, "Who will be here for the children when I am gone?"

Antiretroviral drugs (ARVs) can delay the progression of HIV to AIDS. The drugs were originally so expensive that only the rich could afford them, but the price has come down. The drugs have effectively allowed people who are HIV positive to lead longer, healthier lives. The challenge for developing countries is to make these drugs affordable and available. There is hope for families like the mother and daughter pictured below as the fight against AIDS continues.

The author with Stella, one of her sponsored children.

My family and I have been sponsoring Stella* since 2000. When she was seven, her father passed away and her family had to find cheaper housing far from the Compassion project. Stella now takes a *matatu* every Saturday to the church which offers Bible training, tutoring, training in life skills, and a hot meal. Now, Stella's mother is ill with the disease that becomes the social scourge of the afflicted. The Compassion project helps financially with the medication her mother needs daily. We visited them in Nairobi in 2006. What a highlight to see how financial help through Compassion makes a difference for a whole family.
*name changed

Stella and her mother enjoy opening a bag of gifts from the author.

Internet Links: Visit **Online Resource for HIV AIDS in Africa** at the Aids in Africa website and see People Charts and Epidemic Charts for AIDS statistics which can be understood. AIDS explained to kids at **Kids Health HIV/AIDS** These and more sites at donnaward.net

 View *Africa, A Land of Hope:* Episode 10–A Picture of Care.

What Can I Do?

Read *Ryan and Jimmy and the Well in Africa That Brought Them Together.*

At six years old, Ryan Hreljac wanted to help others less fortunate. When he started saving money for a well in Africa, his perseverance and enthusiasm rippled outward to gain worldwide attention. The money he raised for one well in Uganda has multiplied to two hundred and forty wells by 2006. The effort that started with one child has now helped 400,000 people. A loving heart can touch a multitude.

> Helen Keller said, I am only one but still I am one. I cannot do everything but still I can do something. I will not refuse to do the something I can do.

Financial aid has poured into Africa in the past twenty-five years, but overall, the continent is in greater poverty than ever before. What went wrong? This was the question asked of the *Commission for Africa* in 2004, a committee formed by the British Prime Minister, Mr. Tony Blair. In the final report titled "Our Common Interest," the Commission for Africa stated that well-meaning rich countries and organizations have sometimes brought solutions which are neither good for Africa nor fit in with African culture. The consensus was that it was time for Africans to lead the way in finding answers to their problems. The rich nations should stop and listen, empower the African people, and not come with solutions which may not work within the culture.

How then do you and I help? Problems in Africa are extremely complicated, but the solutions must come from Africans themselves and dependency must be reduced. The greatest benefit of a short missions trip, or *exposure* trip as it is better described, is that the eyes of the rich are opened and their life values often change so that they desire to be contributors instead of consumers. There are many organizations which offer aid to developing countries, but each should be examined regarding their methods and integrity. You should support organizations which encourage self-sufficiency, not dependency. Children need to be given skills which will sustain them in the future. The unemployed young adults need to gain expertise, not buildings. They need to be empowered, not supplied. They need to recognize problems and resolve them, not be given a scheme of solutions.

Whenever possible, nationals should be empowered to do the work instead of foreigners. Nationals know the culture and the costs are far less. It is wise to remember that while aid is vitally important, not all humanitarian aid is helpful.

In a 2005 interview, Kenyan economics expert, James Shikwati, 35, said that aid to Africa does more harm than good.
Journalist: In the West, there are many compassionate citizens wanting to help Africa. Each year, they donate money and pack their old clothes into collection bags....
Shikwati: Why do we get these mountains of clothes? No one is freezing here. Instead, our tailors lose their livelihoods. They're in the same position as our farmers (who cannot compete with donated food). No one in the low-wage world of Africa can be cost-efficient enough to keep pace with donated products. In 1997, 137,000 workers were employed in Nigeria's textile industry. By 2003, the figure had dropped to 57,000. The results are the same in other areas where overwhelming helpfulness and fragile African markets collide.[1]

Humanitarian aid damages the textile industry in Africa.

1 www.spiegel.de/international/spiegel/0,1518,363663,00.html. Accessed 20/11/06.

  Work on completing your Africa notebook including the review on page 60. Plan a day to present your notebook to someone. Talk with your family about things you can do to help others that will bring lasting good.

Political Map of Africa

Africa, A Land of Hope...Resources
© 2006, Donna Ward

Biomes of Africa

Desert

Sahel

Sahel

Savanna

Savanna

Rainforest

Desert

Desert

Savanna

Topographical Map of Africa

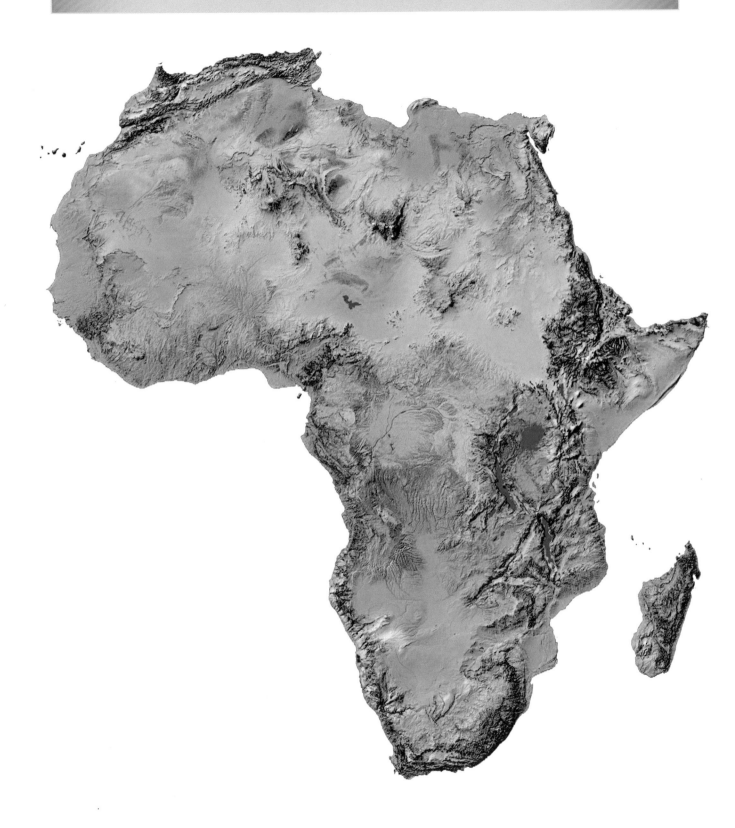

Africa, A Land of Hope...Resources

Country Facts

Country Name:_____

The Land

Total Area: _____

Terrain: _____

Products: _____

_____

Government

Capital City: _____

Leader:_____

Colonial Rule: _____

Date of Independence: _____

The People

Population: _____

Official Languages:_____

_____

Average Life Expectancy: _____

Literacy Rate of Total Population: _____

Interesting Facts or Issues: _____

_____

_____

_____

Famous Places

Landmarks: _____

_____

_____

Other: _____

_____

_____

_____

_____

Flag

Animal Facts

Animal Name: _____

Habitat: _____

Social or Solitary: _____

Carnivore or Herbivore: _____

Threats to Existence: _____

Interesting Facts: _____

_____

_____

_____

_____

_____

Picture

Facts About People

Name:_____

Location:_____

Time Period:_____

Interesting Facts:_____

_____

_____

_____

_____

_____

_____

Picture

What Have I Learned?

Places I liked the best: _____

Why: _____

_____

Person/People I liked the best: _____

Why: _____

_____

Animal I liked the best: _____

Why: _____

_____

Favorite story: _____

Favorite film: _____

Favorite website: _____

Number of African countries I can name and locate: _____

Things I learned about wealth and poverty: _____

_____

Other things I learned: _____

_____

_____

_____

_____

Please send feedback about your experiences through this program: what you liked, what you didn't like, new titles, films or websites you would like to share with others and any other comments to info@donnaward.net

Africa, A Land of Hope...Resources
© 2006, Donna Ward

SPONSORSHIP

Sponsorship is an exciting way to respond to the needs of the impoverished. It is especially productive in empowering Africans to help Africans. If you choose to sponsor with Compassion, please use this form or sponsor online at **donnaward.net—Compassion link.** Tracking sponsorships helps us evaluate possibilites for future publications. Our family sponsors a number of children with Compassion because we have seen the success of this program. We hope to do more. May all your charitable givings, wherever you place them, bring you much joy in the Lord as you store up treasures in heaven.

Transform
the Life of a Child

CANADIAN SPONSORSHIP FORM

▶ **CONTACT INFORMATION**

Name: _____ Date of Birth: M M D D Y Y
For Demographic Purposes

Address: _____

City: _____ Province: _____ Postal Code: _____

Home Phone No.:( )_____ Business Phone:( )_____

E-mail Address: _____

If Under 18 Parent Signature Required: _____ Issue Tax Receipt to: _____
Receipts will be issued to account/card holder's name

▶ **CHILD PREFERENCE**

2878

I prefer a: ☐ **Boy** ☐ **Girl** ☐ **Either**
My area of preference is: ☐ **Africa** ☐ **Asia** ☐ **South America** ☐ **Middle America** ☐ **Any**

▶ **CHILD SPONSORSHIP $35/MTH** — **PLEASE CHOOSE 1 OF THE FOLLOWING PAYMENT OPTIONS**

A **PRE-AUTHORIZED MONTHLY BANK WITHDRAWAL** — A preferred method, saving on administrative costs.

☐ I authorize Compassion Canada to withdraw $35 from my bank account on the ☐ **5th** or ☐ **15th** of the month. (choose one)
Please enclose a void cheque or fill out bank info: Transit#: ___ ___ ___ ___ ___ Bank Code: ___ ___ ___
Account #:_____ Name of Account Holder:_____

☐ For current sponsors — Please add the above donation to my current automatic withdrawal.

B **MONTHLY CREDIT CARD WITHDRAWAL** (Visa or Master Card) — Please provide your credit information below.

☐ I authorize Compassion Canada to debit my credit card in the amount of $35* on the **25th** of each month.
☐ For current sponsors — Please add the above donation to my current automatic withdrawal.
*****PLEASE NOTE:** If we are unable to withdraw your donation on the **25th**, we will retry within the next 5 business days.

Card Number   Expiry Date
☐ **VISA** ☐ **MasterCard** | | | | | | | | | | | | | | | | | | | | | | | |

Name as it appears on credit card:_____

Mailing Address:
Compassion Canada
Box 5591, London, ON N6A 5G8
Tel:800.563.5437•Fax: 866.685.1107
All donations are tax receiptable.

▶ **SIGNATURE REQUIRED**

Signature:_____

Print Name:_____

Compassion
Releasing children from poverty
in Jesus' name

DONNA WARD
NORTHWOODS PRESS

SPONSORSHIP

Sponsorship is an exciting way to respond to the needs of the impoverished. It is especially productive in empowering Africans to help Africans. If you choose to sponsor with Compassion, please use this form or sponsor online at **donnaward.net—Compassion link.** Tracking sponsorships helps us evaluate possibilites for future publications. Our family sponsors a number of children with Compassion because we have seen the success of this program. We hope to do more. May all your charitable givings, wherever you place them, bring you much joy in the Lord as you store up treasures in heaven.

Transform
the Life of a Child
AMERICAN SPONSORSHIP FORM

▶ **CONTACT INFORMATION**

Name: _____ Date of Birth: [M][M][D][D][Y][Y]
For Demographic Purposes

Address: _____

City: _____ State: _____ Zip Code: _____

Home Phone No.:(____) _____ Business Phone:(____) _____

E-mail Address: _____

If Under 18 Parent Signature Required: _____ Issue Tax Receipt to: _____
Receipts will be issued to account/card holder's name

▶ **CHILD PREFERENCE**

I prefer a: ☐ **Boy** ☐ **Girl** ☐ **Either**

My area of preference is: ☐ **Africa** ☐ **Asia** ☐ **South America** ☐ **Middle America** ☐ **Any**

2878

▶ **CHILD SPONSORSHIP $32/MTH** — PLEASE CHOOSE 1 OF THE FOLLOWING PAYMENT OPTIONS

A PRE-AUTHORIZED MONTHLY BANK WITHDRAWAL — A preferred method, saving on administrative costs.

☐ I authorize Compassion to withdraw **$32** from my bank account on the ☐ 5th ☐ 10th ☐ 15th ☐ 20th of the month. (choose one)

Please enclose a void cheque or fill out bank info: Routing#: __ __ __ __ __ __ __ __ __

Account#: __ __ __ __ __ __ __ __ __ __ __ Name of Account Holder:_____

☐ For current sponsors — Please add the above donation to my current automatic withdrawal.

B MONTHLY CREDIT CARD WITHDRAWAL — Please provide your credit information below.

☐ I authorize Compassion to debit my credit card in the amount of **$32*** each month.

☐ For current sponsors — Please add the above donation to my current automatic withdrawal.

***PLEASE NOTE:** If we are unable to withdraw your donation, we will retry within the next 5 business days.*

Card Number   Expiry Date

☐ **VISA** ☐ **MasterCard** ☐ **AMERICAN EXPRESS Card** ☐ **DISCOVER** [| | | | | | | | | | | | | | | | |] [| | | |]

Name as it appears on credit card:_____

Mailing address:
Compassion International
Colorado Springs, CO 80997
Tel: 800.336.7676

▶ **SIGNATURE REQUIRED**

Signature:_____

Print Name:_____

Releasing children from poverty
Compassion
in Jesus' name

DONNA WARD
NORTHWOODS PRESS

SPONSORSHIP

Sponsorship is an exciting way to respond to the needs of the impoverished. It is especially productive in empowering Africans to help Africans. If you choose to sponsor with Compassion, please use this form or sponsor online at **donnaward.net—Compassion link.** Tracking sponsorships helps us evaluate possibilites for future publications. Our family sponsors a number of children with Compassion because we have seen the success of this program. We hope to do more. May all your charitable givings, wherever you place them, bring you much joy in the Lord as you store up treasures in heaven.

Transform
the Life of a Child

CANADIAN SPONSORSHIP FORM

▶ **CONTACT INFORMATION**

Name: _____ Date of Birth: |M|M|D|D|Y|Y|
For Demographic Purposes

Address: _____

City: _____ Province: _____ Postal Code: _____

Home Phone No.:( )_____ Business Phone:( )_____

E-mail Address: _____

If Under 18 Parent Signature Required: _____ Issue Tax Receipt to: _____
Receipts will be issued to account/card holder's name

▶ **CHILD PREFERENCE** | 2878 |

I prefer a: ☐ **Boy** ☐ **Girl** ☐ **Either**

My area of preference is: ☐ **Africa** ☐ **Asia** ☐ **South America** ☐ **Middle America** ☐ **Any**

▶ **CHILD SPONSORSHIP $35/MTH** — **PLEASE CHOOSE 1 OF THE FOLLOWING PAYMENT OPTIONS**

A PRE-AUTHORIZED MONTHLY BANK WITHDRAWAL — A preferred method, saving on administrative costs.

☐ I authorize Compassion Canada to withdraw $35 from my bank account on the ☐ **5ᵗʰ** or ☐ **15ᵗʰ** of the month. (choose one)

Please enclose a void cheque or fill out bank info: Transit#: __ __ __ __ __ Bank Code: __ __ __

Account #:_____ Name of Account Holder:_____

☐ For current sponsors — Please add the above donation to my current automatic withdrawal.

B MONTHLY CREDIT CARD WITHDRAWAL (Visa or Master Card) — Please provide your credit information below.

☐ I authorize Compassion Canada to debit my credit card in the amount of $35★ on the **25ᵗʰ** of each month.

☐ For current sponsors — Please add the above donation to my current automatic withdrawal.

★**PLEASE NOTE:** If we are unable to withdraw your donation on the **25ᵗʰ**, we will retry within the next 5 business days.

Card Number   Expiry Date

☐ **VISA** ☐ **MasterCard** |__|__|__|__|__|__|__|__|__|__|__|__|__|__|__|__| |__|__|__|__|

Name as it appears on credit card:_____

Mailing Address:
Compassion Canada
Box 5591, London, ON N6A 5G8
Tel:800.563.5437•Fax: 866.685.1107
All donations are tax receiptable.

▶ **SIGNATURE REQUIRED**

Signature:_____

Print Name:_____

Releasing children from poverty
Compassion
in Jesus' name

D O N N A   W A R D
NORTHWOODS PRESS

SPONSORSHIP

Sponsorship is an exciting way to respond to the needs of the impoverished. It is especially productive in empowering Africans to help Africans. If you choose to sponsor with Compassion, please use this form or sponsor online at **donnaward.net—Compassion link.** Tracking sponsorships helps us evaluate possibilites for future publications. Our family sponsors a number of children with Compassion because we have seen the success of this program. We hope to do more. May all your charitable givings, wherever you place them, bring you much joy in the Lord as you store up treasures in heaven.

Transform
the Life of a Child

AMERICAN SPONSORSHIP FORM

▶ CONTACT INFORMATION

Name: _____ Date of Birth: | M | M | D | D | Y | Y |
For Demographic Purposes

Address: _____

City: _____ State: _____ Zip Code: _____

Home Phone No.:(____) _____ Business Phone:(____) _____

E-mail Address: _____

If Under 18 Parent Signature Required: _____ Issue Tax Receipt to: _____
Receipts will be issued to account/card holder's name

▶ CHILD PREFERENCE

2878

I prefer a: ☐ **Boy** ☐ **Girl** ☐ **Either**

My area of preference is: ☐ **Africa** ☐ **Asia** ☐ **South America** ☐ **Middle America** ☐ **Any**

▶ CHILD SPONSORSHIP $32/MTH — PLEASE CHOOSE 1 OF THE FOLLOWING PAYMENT OPTIONS

A   PRE-AUTHORIZED MONTHLY BANK WITHDRAWAL — A preferred method, saving on administrative costs.

☐ I authorize Compassion to withdraw $32 from my bank account on the ☐ **5th** ☐ **10th** ☐ **15th** ☐ **20th** of the month. (choose one)

Please enclose a void cheque or fill out bank info: Routing#: __ __ __ __ __ __ __ __ __

Account#: __ __ __ __ __ __ __ __ __ __ __   Name of Account Holder:_____

☐ For current sponsors — Please add the above donation to my current automatic withdrawal.

B   MONTHLY CREDIT CARD WITHDRAWAL — Please provide your credit information below.

☐ I authorize Compassion to debit my credit card in the amount of $32* each month.

☐ For current sponsors — Please add the above donation to my current automatic withdrawal.

***PLEASE NOTE:** If we are unable to withdraw your donation, we will retry within the next 5 business days.*

Card Number   Expiry Date

☐ VISA   ☐ MasterCard   ☐ American Express   ☐ DISCOVER | | | | | | | | | | | | | | | | | | | | | | | | |

Name as it appears on credit card:_____

Mailing address:
Compassion International
Colorado Springs, CO 80997
Tel: 800.336.7676

▶ SIGNATURE REQUIRED

Signature:_____

Print Name:_____

Compassion
Releasing children from poverty
in Jesus' name

DONNA WARD
NORTHWOODS PRESS